Did You Know:

Fascinating Facts and

The Civil War in North Carolina

by J.C. Knowles

Best always!

J.C. Knowles

ISBN-10: 1-944622-18-9

ISBN-13: 978-1-944622-18-9

REALIZATION PRESS

Cover photo credit: Ted Nigrelli
Flicker http://bit.ly/1sN2GE0

Table of Contents

Acknowledgements

Mr. Knowles has spent a lifetime studying the history of North Carolina and filing bits and pieces of special interest on his countless note cards. He acknowledges and thanks the following resources:

The extensive files of *The News and Observer*

Many editions of *Our State* magazine

Chronology of North Carolina by D.K. Bennett (1858; New York; Published by James M. Edney)

Williamson's *History of North Carolina*

The Civil War by Day

North Carolina: History of a Southern State by Hugh Lefler

North Carolina Through Four Hundred Years by William Powell

North Carolina Governors by Beth Crabtree

North Carolina Almanac

Various Booklets on North Carolina

Wake: History of the Capitol County by Elizabeth Reid Murray

J.C. Knowles

Ashe's History of North Carolina

History of Carolina Power and Light Company

County History Series by North Carolina Publications, Division of Cultural Resources

North Carolina Lighthouses by David Stick

Triumph at Kitty Hawk by Tom Parrimore

Foreword

This little booklet is not intended to be a scholarly treatise. Rather, it is a book that might invoke lively discussion and healthy debate. It may have the further effect of dredging up either pleasant or unpleasant memories, but it contains something of interest for anyone who loves the state of North Carolina as deeply as the author, J.C. Knowles.

Mr. Knowles is widely known as a lover of history, a spinner of tall (and short) tales, a speaker at countless banquets that celebrate North Carolina's colorful history, a popular tour leader at the State Capitol, and a regular host at the Raleigh Visitor's Center. He hosts a weekly television show on antiques and has been collecting these snippets of history during his lifetime.

Enjoy!

Ann Huckenbeck, Ph.D.,

Editor

Chapter 1
Fascinating Facts

DID YOU KNOW?

In 1840 the Southern Baptists sent the first foreign missionary from North Carolina to China.

The First Baptist Church on the corner of Salisbury and Edenton streets in Raleigh was completed in 1859.

The Catholic Cemetery on Tarboro Road in Raleigh was established in 1858.

The first military camp in North Carolina was Camp Ellis, located on the State Fairgrounds in Raleigh in 1861. The camp was named in honor of the sitting governor John Ellis.

The first North Carolina troops to leave for combat duty in the Civil War were the First North Carolina Regiment of Volunteers, who left North Carolina on May 21, 1861, headed for Virginia.

Dr. Charles E. Johnson was appointed surgeon general of the North Carolina Confederate troops on May 16, 1861.

North Carolina's first military hospital was established in May 1861 at the Fairground Camp (Camp Ellis); Dr. E. Burke Haywood was the administrator of the facility.

The Pettigrew Hospital, established in 1864, was the largest military hospital in the state. It was located at the corner of Tarboro Road and New Bern Avenue. The hospital was named in honor of General James J. Pettigrew who was killed in action at Gettysburg.

The Main Building at Wake Forest College was placed into service as a Confederate hospital in January 1864. This was Wake County's fourth general hospital.

North Carolina was the only Confederate state that clothed her own troops.

Poet George Moses Hinton, formerly of Northampton County, was the first black professional man of letters in the United States.

The first volume of North Carolina poetry was published in Raleigh in 1810.

A Military and Agriculture College was introduced in the General Assembly in 1826. The college was to be in Wake County. The military committee tabled the bill in 1827.

The first church located in Wake County was the Middle Creek Baptist Church, established in 1756 or earlier.

The United States Government established the United States National Military Cemetery in Raleigh in 1866 on the grounds of the former Rock Quarry Cemetery.

The first Hebrew Cemetery in Raleigh was established in 1870.

The *Deaf Mute Casket*, a newspaper for the deaf, began publication in Raleigh in 1860.

In 1866, Shaw University in Raleigh became the first Negro institution in America to enroll women.

Commercial airline service began in Raleigh in September 1929.

In 1930, 88 banks in North Carolina failed as did 232 Building and Loan Associations.

On March 14, 1932 Dr. Frank Porter Graham became the first president of the consolidated University of North Carolina system.

In 1938 the School of Engineering was transferred from the University of North Carolina to North Carolina State in Raleigh.

The State Legislature created the North Carolina State Board of Health on February 12, 1877.

During the term of Governor O. Max Gardner (1919-33), state employees' salaries were reduced by 20% and under Governor J.C.B. Ehringhaus (1933-37), salaries were reduced another 25%.

Cotton farmers in North Carolina witnessed a drastic drop in price of this important "cash crop" in 1932 from 30 cents a pound to six and one-half cents per pound!

In an examination of 140,000 school children in 41 counties in 1929 and 1930, public health officials found that 23,000 suffered from malnutrition.

When families found food hard to obtain during the depression in North Carolina, they ate dandelion and pokeweed leaves for their daily diet of greens.

The Citizens Conservation Corp (CCC) was established in March 1933 to provide jobs for single men between the ages of 17 and 25.

The Rural Electrification Administration (REA) was established in North Carolina in May 1935.

The National Recovery Administration (NRA) was established in North Carolina in June 1933.

North Carolina created the Unemployment Compensation Commission in 1926.

During the administration of President Franklin Roosevelt, the Social Security System was implemented in North Carolina in 1935.

Under the aegis of Governor Clyde Hoey (1937-41), tourism in North Carolina grew from 36 million dollars annually to 102 million dollars.

Four hundred and fifty thousand men between the ages of 21 and 36 registered in North Carolina after the Selective Service Act was approved in 1940.

Construction on Cherry Point Marine Air Station began in July 1941; the base officially opened in March 1942.

Camp Davis, an anti-aircraft and artillery training base in Onslow County, opened in April 1941.

Seymour Johnson Air Base at Goldsboro was established in 1941 as an Army Air Force Technical Training School.

Construction on Camp Lejeune Marine Base began in 1942.

During World War II, more fighting men were trained in North Carolina than in any other state.

In 1944 the North Carolina Pharmaceutical Association sold war bonds to purchase five ambulance planes. The drive was successful, raising over $2.3 million.

The first woman to command a major Army Medical Corps was Dr. Margaret O. Craighill of Southport.

During World War II North Carolina had 258,000 men and women in the Army, 90,000 in the Navy and 13,000 in the Marine Corps. Of the total, 4,088 were killed in action.

North Carolina inaugurated the nine-month school year in 1944. The 12th grade of school was added the same year.

Poliomyelitis (Polio) struck 2,498 people in North Carolina during 1948.

North Carolina Memorial Hospital in Chapel Hill opened in 1952.

The University of North Carolina created the Division of Health Affairs in 1947.

In 1949 the School of Dentistry and Nursing opened at the University of North Carolina.

The North Carolina Museum of Art opened in a building in downtown Raleigh in 1956.

Black students were admitted to the University of North Carolina Schools of Law, Medicine and other graduate programs for the first time in 1951.

In 1957 schools in Charlotte, Greensboro and Winston Salem became the first integrated schools in the state.

Henry E. Frye, a native of Ellerbe, was the first black to be elected to the North Carolina House of Representatives in 1968. Today (year 2001) he sits as the Chief Justice of the North Carolina Supreme Court.

Research Triangle Park, the brainchild of Governor Luther Hodges, was incorporated in December 1958.

The first known casualty in the Vietnam War was Air Force Technical Sergeant Floyd Milton Frazer from Waynesville who was killed in February 1962.

In 1972 Richard Epps of Wilmington became the first black student to be elected president of the student body at the University of North Carolina.

The "Speaker Ban Law," enacted in North Carolina on June 26, 1963, prohibited any known Communist from speaking on a campus of the University of North Carolina system.

In 1911 North Carolina began to purchase land containing the headwaters of certain rivers to protect the water supply in the state.

In 1971 there were 1,900 crimes per 100,000 persons in North Carolina; the national average was 2,800.

At the request of Governor James B. Hunt, Jr., the Department of Crime Control was established in 1977 by the General Assembly.

In 1987 the State of North Carolina budgeted $262 million to maintain its 85 prisons.

The North Carolina General Assembly met for the first time in the new Legislative Building on Jones Street in Raleigh in 1963.

In 1965 State College in Raleigh was renamed North Carolina State University, and Charlotte College became the University of North Carolina at Charlotte. In 1969, there were more changes: Asheville-Biltmore College became the University of North Carolina at Asheville and Wilmington College became the University of North Carolina at Wilmington.

In 1971 the remaining ten state-supported institutions of higher learning were brought under the umbrella of the University of North Carolina system.

Educational television (UNC-TV) began in North Carolina on January 8, 1955 with studios on the campus of the University of North Carolina at Chapel Hill.

The Community College System was established in North Carolina in 1957.

A grant from the Richardson Foundation in 1963 enabled establishment of the North Carolina Film Board.

The North Carolina Art Museum on Blue Ridge Road in Raleigh opened in 1983.

In 1973 James E. Holshouser became the first Republican elected governor of North Carolina in the 1900's.

Although the Women's Suffrage Amendment became part of the United States Constitution on August 26, 1920, North Carolina did not ratify the amendment until 1971.

The State Constitution was amended in 1977 to allow a governor to serve two successive terms.

In 1900 there were 660,000 school-age children in North Carolina. However, only about two-thirds were enrolled in school and less than half attended on a regular basis.

Within a year after the Rural High School Act was adopted in 1907, nearly 160 high schools were opened in North Carolina.

By the mid 1920's North Carolina had more school children riding buses to and from school than any other state in the country.

Between 1889 and 1936 there were 68 lynchings in North Carolina.

The North Carolina General Assembly authorized the creation of the North Carolina Historical Commission on March 9, 1903.

On March 9, 1915 the North Carolina General Assembly created Mount Mitchell State Park.

As early as 1852 in North Carolina a group of over 20,000 signed a petition calling on the legislature to seek statewide Prohibition. The movement failed.

During the Civil War it was against the law in North Carolina to use grain to distill whiskey on grounds that grain was needed for food.

By popular vote, in 1908 North Carolina became the first state in the nation to banish liquor traffic by popular vote.

The Knights of Labor organized the first assembly in the state in Raleigh in 1884.

The General Assembly adopted the first child labor law in North Carolina in 1903.

When the United States declared war against Germany on April 6, 1917, it was called "the war to end all wars."

During World War I, North Carolina sent 86, 457 men to war. Of this number 20,350 were black. There were 195 nurses from the state. Losses included 629 killed in action, 204 dead from wounds and 1,542 perished from disease.

The North Carolina Grange was incorporated in 1875.

Leonidas L. Polk established the Progressive Farmer, a weekly newspaper with farm interest in 1886.

The North Carolina College of Agriculture and Mechanic Arts (NCSU today), opened in Raleigh in 1889.

The North Carolina Railroad Commission was established by the General Assembly in 1889.

From 1868 to 1899 New Hanover County had the most blacks in the State Legislature with nine. A total of 127 blacks served during this time.

In 1897 over 1,000 blacks served in the legislature either by election or by appointment.

The worse race riot in the state's history occurred in Wilmington on November 10, 1898. Democrats were fearful that blacks would rule throughout the state.

The Grand Lodge of Masons in North Carolina established, in 1873, the Oxford Orphanage (changed to Masonic Home for Children at Oxford) in Granville County.

A state-supported "Colored Orphanage" at Oxford was established in 1883.

The Insane Asylum (Dorothea Dix Hospital) was established in Raleigh in 1853; Western North Carolina Insane Asylum opened in Morganton in 1875; and the "Colored" Insane Asylum in Goldsboro opened in 1877.

Horse-drawn streetcars began operations in Raleigh and Wilmington in 1887.

In 1896 mail was carried from the post office to residents on rural routes in China Grove, the first rural delivery service in North Carolina.

On May 11, 1898, Worth Bagley of Raleigh became the first American Naval Officer killed in the Spanish-American War.

The state motto Esse Quam Videri (To Be Rather Than to Seem) was adopted in 1893.

The first cotton mill in North Carolina, the Schenck Cotton Mill in Lincoln County, was built in 1813.

Thomasville, known as the "Chair City of the South," had one of its furniture factories producing as many as 1,500 chairs per day in 1907.

As early as 1900 North Carolina had over 3,800 miles of railroad.

In 1860 North Carolina farmers produced 145,000 bales of cotton and 33,000,000 pounds of tobacco. Forty years later (1900), the figures were 480,000 bales of cotton and 123,000,000 pounds of tobacco.

The State Constitution of 1868 required that a system of free public schools be established.

In 1877 the General Assembly created the Fayetteville Colored Normal School (now Fayetteville State University) as a teacher-training institution for blacks.

The first summer school ever held at a college or university in the United States, opened at the University of North Carolina in 1877.

In 1880 about one-third of the state's school-age children attended school for the nine weeks of instruction offered at their local school.

Due to financial restraints, the University of North Carolina closed the school in 1870 and did not reopen until 1875.

In 1865 Wake Forest Institute (Wake Forest University), Davidson College and Trinity College (Duke University) closed their doors to students because of the effects of the Civil War. The schools reopened the following year.

On May 29, 1865 President Andrew Johnson appointed William Woods Holden Provisional Governor of North Carolina.

In the spring of 1867 President Andrew Johnson attended commencement exercises at the University of North Carolina.

The Republican Party in North Carolina was organized on March 27, 1867 in the Capitol's House of Representatives with 101 white delegates and 46 black delegates attending.

The membership of the North Carolina Constitutional Convention that met in 1867 was as follows: 107 Republicans, 18 Carpetbaggers, 15 Blacks and 74 Native Whites.

Section Four of the North Carolina Constitution of 1867 declared, "North Carolina would henceforth remain a member of the American nation without right to secede."

In 1866 six young Confederate veterans met in Pulaski, Tennessee in the law office of Thomas N. Jones, a native of Person County, North Carolina and formed the Ku Klux Klan.

When the Republican Party of North Carolina was organized, it was said: "The party was composed in large measure of carpetbaggers, blacks and scalawags."

On March 5, 1869 the General Assembly approved an act "guaranteeing the right to vote to all citizens regardless of race, color or previous condition of servitude."

Editor Josiah Turner, Jr. of the *Raleigh Sentinel* in 1868 called the members of the Republican-controlled General Assembly, "a minstrel of ignorant Negroes and greedy carpetbaggers and scalawags."

On February 26, 1870 in Graham (Alamance County), a large band of robed horsemen entered the home of Wyatt Outlaw, a black Republican leader, abducted him, and took him to the town square where he was hanged.

On April 20, 1861 a company of Charlotte Grays seized the United States Mint in that city and on April 22, the United States Army Captain in charge of the Federal Arsenal at Fayetteville surrendered to the rebels.

In 1862 North Carolina purchased four steamships to be sent to England to sell cotton and buy supplies for North Carolina troops.

Though most medicines for North Carolina's Confederate troops were imported, there was a medical laboratory near Lincolnton, operated by Dr. A. S. Piggott.

Prior to Lincoln's issuing the Emancipation Proclamation on July 1, 1863, the Union was fighting for the preservation of the Union only. After the proclamation, however, the North considered the battle was not only for the preservation of the Union but also for the freeing of the slaves.

Of the 15, 301 Confederate soldiers killed in the Battle of Gettysburg, 4,033 were North Carolinians.

The Confederate Ram *Albemarle* was destroyed on October 27, 1864 on the Roanoke River near Plymouth.

During the War Between the States, the ship *Shenandoah* traveled around the world. Captain James Iredell Waddell, a native of Pittsboro, Chatham County, commanded the ship and destroyed Union supplies valued at $1,172,223.

During the 1945 winter season in North Carolina, there were 61 snows and the lowest temperature in the state was six below zero.

The Village of Salem received two fire engines from Europe on May 9, 1785.

The Methodists held their first conference at Green Hill in Franklin County on April 19, 1785.

Florida's first elected governor was a native of North Carolina. William Dunn Moseley was born in Lenoir County on February 1, 1795. He moved to Florida around 1835 and was elected Governor on June 25, 1845.

The General Assembly passed the following law in 1795: No person shall set up any billiard table or other tables or device for playing at any game of hazard within 5 miles of the University at Chapel Hill. Offenders found guilty shall pay a 50- pound fine.

On November 18, 1805 the State Court of Conference became the North Carolina Supreme Court.

A black slave woman was burned at the stake in 1805 for poisoning four people in Wayne County.

John Jones McRae was born on January 10, 1815 in Anson County. In 1818, he moved to Mississippi and in 1854, was elected Governor of that state.

In 1825 the General Assembly created a fund for the establishment of Common Schools in the state.

Richard J. Gatling, born in Hertford County, North Carolina on September 12, 1818, received a patent for a revolving six-barrel machine gun on November 4, 1862. For many years, his invention was referred to as the "Gatling Gun."

As early as 1622 an expedition from Jamestown, Virginia explored the Chowan River area in Gates County, North Carolina.

The Chowan Baptist Association established Chowan College in 1848 as the Chowan Baptist Female Institute.

Union troops burned the town of Winston in Hertford County on February 20, 1862. This was the first town to be destroyed by fire in North Carolina during the War Between the States.

George Washington visited North Carolina in 1791 during this Southern tour.

Colonel John Barnwell of South Carolina built Fort Barnwell in Craven County in April 1712 during fighting with the Tuscarora Indians.

Union troops built Fort Totten on the outskirts of New Bern following their capture of the town in March 1862.

The Tuscarora Indians executed Henry Lawson, author of *History of North Carolina*, on September 21, 1711.

Manteo, a Hatteras Indian who accompanied John White to England in 1587, was the first Indian baptized into the Protestant faith. Sir Walter Raleigh gave Manteo the title of "Lord of Roanoke."

The Eighth Transportation Battalion, formed April 1, 1954 at Fort Bragg, was the first helicopter battalion.

Lt. Colonel Mattie V. Parker, a native of Mt. Olive, was given command of the Army Recruiting Command's Armed Forces Examining and Entrance Station at Detroit, Michigan on May 31, 1975. She was the first woman to hold such a command in the United States Army.

John White, Governor and leader of Sir Walter Raleigh's voyages, was the first English artist in the New World. He painted watercolors of the North Carolina coast in 1585.

Colonel David Carl Schilling of Raleigh, commanding officer of the 31st Escort Wing, left Manston, England on September 22, 1950 and made the first jet transatlantic nonstop flight from East to West. After flying 3,300 miles, Schilling landed his single-engine F-84E Republic Thunderjet at the Air Force Base, Limestone, Maine.

Richard Caswell became the first governor of the State of North Carolina in 1776.

North Carolina has 301 miles of coastline.

Bath, the oldest town in North Carolina, was incorporated in 1703.

North Carolina has about 37,000 miles of freshwater streams.

North Carolina has 1,500 lakes of 10 acres or more.

There are 17 major river basins in North Carolina.

Mt. Mitchell is the state's highest peak: 6,684 feet.

North Carolina is the leading manufacturer of tobacco, textiles and brick, and markets the most furniture of any state in the United States.

The New River, located in the Appalachian Mountains of Ashe County, is the oldest river the nation and the second oldest in the world.

The tallest natural sand dune on the east coast is Jockey's Ridge at Nags Head; it stands 137 feet high.

The Cape Hatteras Lighthouse on North Carolina's Outer Banks is 208 feet tall and is the tallest lighthouse in the United States.

The Venus Flytrap, which eats and digests insects and other small living things, survives only in an approximate 100-mile area located near Wilmington.

Virginia Dare was the first white child of English parents born in America. She was born on Roanoke Island on August 18, 1587.

Orville and Wilbur Wright piloted man's first successful flight in an airplane at Kitty Hawk, North Carolina on December 17, 1903.

The first armed resistance against the British Crown was in November 1765 at Brunswick Town, North Carolina.

On April 12, 1776 the Halifax Resolves authorized North Carolina delegates to the Continental Congress to declare Independence from England, making this the first colony in the nation to do so.

President George Washington appointed James Iredell of Edenton, North Carolina to the first United States Supreme Court.

The North Carolina General Assembly chartered the University of North Carolina on December 11, 1789. The University opened on January 15, 1795 and was the first state-supported university in the United States.

A deed was signed on April 5, 1792 purchasing 1,000 acres of land in Wake County from Joel Lane; it was the site upon which the "City of Raleigh" was plotted.

Fire destroyed the State House (State Capitol) in Raleigh on June 21, 1831.

The first public meeting to promote railroads in North Carolina was held in Alamance County on August 1, 1828.

David Fanning and his Tories captured Governor Thomas Burke in Hillsborough on September 12, 1781.

Governor William Tryon defeated the Regulators at the Battle of Alamance on May 16, 1771.

General Joseph E. Johnston surrendered his army to General William T. Sherman at the Bennett House in Durham County on April 26, 1865.

Central Orphanage of North Carolina, a pioneer "Negro" child-caring institution, was founded in 1883 at Oxford.

The Confederate Army established a cemetery at Kittrell in Vance County. Graves of 52 soldiers who died in the Kittrell Springs Hotel Hospital 1864-65 are located there.

Thomas O. Larkin was U.S. Consul at Monterey, California, 1844-1848. His home was in Duplin County.

During the War Between the States, there was an arms factory in Kenansville, Duplin County. It manufactured bowie knives, bayonets and small arms.

The home of Confederate General William D. Pender, killed in the battle at Gettysburg, was in Wilson County.

East Carolina University, formerly known as East Carolina Teachers College, was established in 1907. It became a four-year school in 1920 and a university in 1967.

The North Carolina Baptist State Convention was organized in Pitt County on March 26, 1830.

The North Carolina Press Association was organized in Goldsboro on May 14, 1873.

Peace College in Raleigh, a Presbyterian high school and junior college for women, was chartered in 1857. It opened officially in 1872 after having served as a Confederate hospital. The college now offers both associate and bachelor's degrees.

The Battle of Bentonville in Johnston County was fought March 19-21, 1865.

The Raleigh Gaston Railroad was chartered in 1835 and completed in 1840. The road was 85 miles long.

Raleigh, the capital city, surrendered to General William T. Sherman on April 13, 1865.

Reverend Aldert Smedes opened Saint Mary's Episcopal School for Girls in Raleigh on May 12, 1842.

Shaw University opened in 1865 as a "School for Negroes."

The voters in Charlotte rejected a tax levy to support the city's Public Library, causing the library to close in 1939.

W.J. Cash hanged himself in a Mexican hotel room in 1941, only five months after publication of his book *The Mind of the South*.

In 1939, Ted McElroy, competing in a contest in Asheville, set a world record for receiving Morse code: 75.2 words per minute.

On July 3, 1929 a monument to North Carolina Civil War dead was dedicated at the Gettysburg Battlefield. Gutzon Borglum sculpted the memorial.

Union cavalry troops destroyed the arms factory at Kenansville, Duplin County on July 4, 1862.

On July 5, 1836 Horace Greeley, a New York newspaperman, married Mary Cheney in Warrenton, North Carolina.

Governor Dan K. Moore dedicated the state's first Welcome Center, on I-85 north of Henderson, on August 1, 1968.

In 1837 the steamship *Home*, while trying to break its own record for speed between New York and Charleston, floundered in a storm off Cape Hatteras. Ninety of the 135 passengers and crew lost their lives.

In 1984 Velma Barfield was executed by lethal injection at Central Prison in Raleigh. She was the first woman executed in the United States in 22 years.

Henry Frye of Guilford County was sworn as a member of the North Carolina House of Representatives on November 5, 1968. He was the first black to serve in this capacity since 1898.

In 1787 future president Andrew Jackson was admitted to the bar in Rowan County.

The prison population at the Confederate Salisbury Prison reached its peak on November 6, 1864 when a prison built to hold 2,600 housed 8,740.

Movie star Ava Gardner was born in Johnston County on December 24, 1922. She married her third husband Frank Sinatra in 1951.

Exum Clement, an Asheville lawyer, was the first woman elected to the North Carolina General Assembly. She was elected in 1921.

President William Taft visited Wilmington in 1909.

On December 1, 1677 some 100-armed rebels, opposing a tax on tobacco not shipped directly to England, seized control in the Albemarle region and put the acting governor on trial.

The Currituck Beach Lighthouse was lit for the first time on December 1, 1875.

The last of the Cherokee Indians left North Carolina for Indian grounds west of the Mississippi in 1838.

Benny and Billy McCrary, born in Hendersonville in 1946, grew up as the heaviest twins in the world. At age 32, Billy weighed 743 pounds and Benny, 723 pounds.

In 1965 over 1,000 students from North Carolina State University stormed the campus newspaper office and demanded that the editor apologize for suggesting that "Dixie" be stricken from the repertoire of campus musical groups.

After three days of shelling, Fort Fisher surrendered to the Union forces on January 15, 1865.

The Stonewall Jackson Training School for troubled youth opened near Concord in 1909. This was one of the first boys' reformatories in the nation.

The first state-supported Common School in North Carolina opened in Rockingham County on January 20, 1840.

Jim Beatty, a native of Charlotte, broke the four-minute mile indoor track record in a time of three minutes and 58.9 seconds at a meet in the Los Angeles Sports Arena on February 10, 1962.

Martin Luther King, Jr. paid his first visit to North Carolina at a rally in Greensboro on February 11, 1958.

The first student to enroll at the University of North Carolina was Hinton James from Wilmington who enrolled on February 12, 1795. Folklore says that James walked the 120 miles distance from Wilmington to Chapel Hill.

On February 13, 1830 in State vs Mann, the North Carolina Supreme Court declined to investigate the circumstances of slavery. Harriet Beecher Stowe would later use the case as a background for *Uncle Tom's Cabin*, her 1852 novel.

James K. Polk, born in Mecklenburg County in 1849, was the first president to have his picture taken in the White House.

In February 1891 the General Assembly approved the establishment of the Soldier's Home for Confederate Veterans that was to be located in Raleigh.

Country singer Donna Fargo was born in Mount Airy, North Carolina in 1949. Her real name was Yvone Vaughan.

On July 15, 1916 Altapass in Mitchell County was hit with 22.22 inches of rain in 24 hours, a state record.

The first soil conservation district in the United States was established in 1937 in Anson County.

In 1918 *The Diamond Shoals Lightship*, moored off Cape Hatteras, was shelled and sunk by a German submarine.

The first Walmart store in North Carolina opened at Murphy in the western part of the state August 16, 1983.

The first forestry school in the nation opened at George Vanderbilt's Biltmore Forest in 1898; German immigrant Carl Schenck served as director.

Hugh Morton, owner of Grandfather Mountain, opened the Mile High Swinging Bridge on September 2, 1952.

Margaret Mitchell and husband Red Upshaw spent their honeymoon in Asheville in 1922. She used Upshaw as a model for the Rhett Butler character in *Gone with the Wind*. Upshaw is buried in Oakwood Cemetery in Raleigh.

Pamlico County School System inaugurated North Carolina's first motorized school bus service in 1917.

In 1802 at New Bern, John Stanly killed Richard Dobbs Spaight, the state's first native-born governor, in a duel provoked by Stanly.

The University of North Carolina closed during the Civil War but reopened for enrollment on September 6, 1875.

On September 11, 1974 Eastern Airline's flight 212 crashed and burned three miles from the Charlotte airport; of the 82 people aboard, 72 lost their lives.

The first train to enter Asheville from across the Blue Ridge Mountains arrived on October 2, 1880. Asheville has been a tourist mecca ever since that date.

The USS *North Carolina* reached its final berth in Wilmington on October 2, 1961.

The Andy Griffith Show, set in fictional Mayberry, North Carolina, premiered on CBS on October 3, 1960.

Duke University dedicated its new 35,000-seat football stadium (Wallace Wade) on October 5, 1929.

On October 8, 1864, Captain James I. Waddell of Pittsboro in Chatham County was assigned by the Confederate Government to do great damage to the Union fleet at sea. His flagship was the *Shenandoah*.

Millie McCoy died at her native home in Columbus County on October 8, 1912. A day later, her Siamese twin sister Christine died.

On October 10, 1934 President Franklin D. Roosevelt appointed University of North Carolina historian R.D.W. Conner, a Wilson native, as the nation's first archivist.

North Carolina required all motor-vehicle drivers to be licensed as of November 1, 1935.

Margaret Sanger gave the South's first public lecture on birth control at Elizabeth City in 1919.

On November 2, 1920 women in North Carolina received the right to vote for the first time in history. They voted in such large numbers that the ballot counting was delayed.

Federal agents captured a 20,000-gallon moonshine still in Wilkes County in 1942.

The towns of Fuquay Springs and Varina merged into one town, Fuquay-Varina, in 1963.

The popular *State* magazine made its debut as a weekly publication in Raleigh on June 3, 1933; its publisher was Carl Goerch.

The famous Forth Fisher hermit, Robert Harrell, died on the beach on June 3, 1972.

In 1835 Catholics won the right to hold office in North Carolina, but free blacks lost the right to vote.

The first Walgreen's Drug Store opened in Charlotte on June 6, 1931.

A textile striker gunned down Police Chief O.F. Aderholt of Gastonia on June 7, 1929.

On March 26, 1852 Dr. William Peter Mallet performed the first caesarean section in the South in which the patient survived.

A company of Charlotte Grays seized the Branch Mint in Charlotte on April 20, 1861.

At the Battle of Big Bethel, Henry Lawson Wyatt of Edgecombe County became the first Confederate soldier killed in action in the War Between the States.

The greatest heavyweight champion of all time, Jack Johnson, was fatally injured in a car accident 25 miles north of Raleigh on June 10, 1946.

Lieutenant William Shipp, born in Asheville and reared in Charlotte and Lincolnton, died on July 1, 1898 while leading his troops up San Juan Hill during the Spanish American War.

The North Carolina Highway Patrol suffered its first highway death one day after the patrol was organized. G.I. Thompson of Marion died when his motorcycle collided with a truck on July 2, 1929.

Althea Gibson, who lived in Wilmington for a number of years, was the first black tennis player to win a singles match at Wimbledon.

Joseph Hewes of Edenton, William Hooper of Hillsborough and John Penn of Stovall signed the Declaration of Independence on August 2, 1776.

The first armed resistance against the British Crown was held on February 19, 1766. Stamp Act protesters in Wilmington, organized as the "Sons of Liberty," marched to Brunswick and forced a British officer to release ships detained for a lack of stamped papers.

James Pinckney Henderson, a native of Lincolnton, was sworn in as the first governor of Texas on February 19, 1846.

On February 20, 1862 the town of Winton in Hertford County became the first North Carolina town to be burned to the ground by Union forces.

In 1915 the North Carolina General Assembly exempted Confederate veterans from jury duty and prohibited white nurses from attending to black patients in North Carolina hospitals.

North Carolina's last surviving Confederate veteran, Samuel E. Bennett of Yancey County, died in 1951 at age 100.

North Carolina's oldest town, Bath, was incorporated in 1905.

On March 11, 1910 Henry Spivey of Elizabethtown, Bladen County was executed for the murder of his father-in-law. His was the last public hanging in North Carolina.

In 1973 Henry Ward Oxendine of Robeson County became the first Native American to be elected to the North Carolina General Assembly.

The first recorded duel in North Carolina occurred on March 18, 1765 at Brunswick between two British Naval officers.

In 1863 the women of Salisbury, most of them wives of Confederate soldiers, armed themselves with axes and went on a search party for food.

James Hutchins of Rutherford County was the first person in North Carolina to be executed by lethal injection. He was convicted of killing three police officers and was executed on March 16, 1984.

Howard Cosell, sportscaster for many years, was born in Winston Salem on March 25, 1920.

Twenty-four tornadoes ripped across North and South Carolina on March 28, 1984; the disasters killed 69, injured over 1,300 and left more than 3,000 homeless.

The *Charlotte Observer* received the Pulitzer Prize in 1988 for its exposure of the misuse of funds by the PTL Club founded by Jim and Tammy Baker.

The historic Goody's Headache Powder Company in Winston Salem closed its doors on March 31, 1995.

The first long-distance telephone call made in North Carolina was made from Raleigh to Wilmington on April 14, 1879.

In 1980 Sally Field won the best-actress Oscar for "Norma Rae," based on the union-organizing effort of Roanoke Rapids textile worker Crystal Lee Sutton.

The longest plank road in the world was located between Fayetteville and Salem in Forsyth County in 1853.

A riot at Central Prison in Raleigh on April 17, 1968 left six inmates dead; among the 78 others wounded in the melee were three guards and two state troopers.

In 1935 the General Assembly made Easter Monday a holiday so state employees could attend the State College and Wake Forest College baseball game. The holiday was switched to Good Friday in 1987.

On April 20, 1989 the Plott hound, native to Haywood County, was named the State dog.

In 1985 the Reverend Sun Myung Moon, founder of the Unification Church, received an honorary degree from Shaw Divinity School in Raleigh.

The trademark "Pepsi Cola" received a patent on June 16, 1903. This popular soft drink had its beginnings in New Bern.

Governor Clyde Hoey dedicated the North Carolina exhibit at the New York World's Fair on June 19, 1939.

Michael Jordan, basketball player at the University of North Carolina, was selected third in the NBA draft of 1984.

On July 11, 1979 the world's largest windmill was dedicated on Howard Knob above Boone.

WBTV in Charlotte was the first television station in the state, signing on the air on July 15, 1949.

Mary Baker Eddy, founder of the Christian Science Church, once lived in Wilmington.

Sir Richard Grenville led the first Sir Walter Raleigh expedition that reached Roanoke Island on July 27, 1585.

In 1988, improper wiring in a control panel sent the $1.2 million, 20-ton scoreboard at the brand-new Charlotte Coliseum crashing to the floor.

On August 16, 1918 a most-daring act of bravery occurred when the members of the life-saving service at Chicamacomico rescued 42 members of the British tanker *Mirlo* that had been hit by a German submarine.

A hurricane with winds of over 135 miles per hour hit the coast of North Carolina on August 18, 1879, but only two lives were lost in the storm.

Charles Carroll and Freeman Gosden, the men who founded the "Amos and Andy Show," first met in Durham.

James Cannon established Cannon Mills in Cabarrus County in 1887.

The North Carolina Transportation Museum opened in the Spencer Shops in Spencer on August 25, 1980.

Dock Rogers, a black man accused of shooting two white people, was lynched in Pender County on August 27, 1933.

On August 30, 1983 William Thompson of Faison became the first North Carolinian in space.

The first National Flag of the Confederate States of America was adopted on March 4, 1861.

The Second Flag of the Confederate States of America was adopted on May 1, 1863 and used for the first time at the funeral of General Stonewall Jackson.

The Third National Flag of the Confederate States of America was adopted on March 4, 1865.

The Confederate Battle Flag "Stars and Bars" was adopted in September 1861.

In 1913 President Woodrow Wilson appointed Josephus Daniels, publisher and editor of the Raleigh *News and Observer*, Secretary of the Navy.

On January 28, 1916 the state's first "double" electrocution claimed a third victim. Ed Walker and Jeff Dorsett were put to death in the electric chair, and as warden T.P. Sales was signing the book declaring both men dead, he himself fell over dead.

On January 3, 1935 the Raleigh City Council passed an ordinance closing the cities' churches and theaters for 10 days to reduce, in some measure, the spread of influenza.

William Gaston's song "The Old North State" was officially adopted as the state song on January 8, 1927.

Rev. M. L. Latta incorporated Latta University in the Oberlin section of Raleigh on January 15, 1894. There were once 28 buildings on this campus.

George W. Graham, M.D. (1847-1923) was the first physician in North Carolina to limit his practice to eyes. Dr. Graham practiced in Raleigh.

The Raleigh City Council, on January 21, 1947, passed an ordinance requiring that fire alarm bells or gongs be placed on every floor in a hotel.

On March 6, 1800 Methodist Bishop Francis Asbury preached to 2,000 souls in the State House on Union Square. Raleigh's population in 1800 was less than 1,000 persons.

When the United States declared war on Germany on April 6, 1917, the Stars and Stripes flew over the Confederate Soldiers Home in Raleigh for the first time since the Civil War. Sixty Confederate veterans volunteered for active service.

The first train to enter Raleigh was the *Tornado*, piloted by engineer Albert Johnson. The train arrived on the newly completed Raleigh-Gaston Railroad on March 20, 1840.

Thomas Wolfe died at age 37 at Johns Hopkins Hospital in Baltimore on September 15, 1938.

A torpedo from a Japanese submarine hit the USS *North Carolina* on September 15, 1942. The ship made it back to Pearl Harbor for repairs.

The Cape Hatteras lighthouse converted from kerosene to electricity in 1934.

Hurricane Hazel hit the coast of North Carolina on October 15, 1954. It was North Carolina's worst hurricane up until that time.

The first State Fair was held in Raleigh on October 18, 1853.

The state's first recognized intercollegiate football game was played on October 18, 1888 at the State Fair Grounds in Raleigh. Wake Forest College defeated the University of North Carolina 6 to 4.

The state's first department store escalators were installed in Efird's Department Store in Charlotte on October 19, 1923.

The daughter of General Robert E. Lee, Anne Carter, died of typhoid fever on October 20, 1862 in Warren County. Anne was a student at Saint Mary's College in Raleigh.

The movie *Sound of Music* played to 247,000 people in Charlotte during a 79-week run.

North Carolina's first public meeting on women's suffrage was held in Asheville on November 15, 1894.

The *Raleigh Register* became the first daily newspaper in North Carolina on November 19, 1850.

On December 21, 1936 Thad Eure of Gates County took office as Secretary of State. He held the office for 52 years, the longest in State history.

The state's first full-time movie theater, *The Bijou*, opened in Wilmington on December 24, 1906.

On December 27, 1892 the nation's first black intercollegiate football was played on a snow-covered field in Salisbury. Livingstone College was beaten 4-0 by Biddle University (now Johnson C. Smith University).

Spivey's Corner, a small community in Sampson County, hosted the first annual National Hollerin' Contest on June 28, 1969.

On June 27, 1857 Dr. Elisha Mitchell fell 40 feet to his death during a climb up Black Mountain in the Blue Ridge. Mt. Mitchell was named in his honor.

Land in Ashe County could be purchased for five cents an acre in 1811.

In 1945, there were 61 snows in North Carolina; the lowest temperature for the year was six below zero.

There is an old legend in Avery County that Frank James, brother of Jesse James, traveled through the county and hid some of his loot there.

On the Town Creek in Brunswick County, a town was established in 1664: Charles Town. After six years, it moved to Charles Town, South Carolina.

In 1860 Brunswick County produced seven million pounds of rice.

The Battery Park Hotel in Asheville was built in 1886 at a cost of over one million dollars.

Fire destroyed the Confederate Hospital in Asheville in 1892.

Buncombe County furnished seven of the ten companies of the 69th North Carolina Regiment during the Civil War.

The Creek Indians migrated near Mt. Gilead in Montgomery County in the 1500's.

An English explorer, Arthur Barlow, was told when he reached North Carolina's shore that a hurricane wrecked a ship on the coast in 1558 and several white men were saved from the wreck.

Queen Elizabeth of England knighted Sir Walter Raleigh on January 6, 1585.

Sir Walter Raleigh was beheaded by order of King James I on October 29, 1618.

In 1651 Edward Bland came from Virginia to explore Carolina; he published a description of the region titled *The Discovery of New Brittaine.*

Nathaniel Batts purchased land from the Yeopin Indians on the Pasquotank River in the northeastern region of the Carolinas in 1657.

On March 24, 1663 Charles II granted Carolina territory to eight Lords Proprietors: Edward Hyde, George Monck, Anthony Ashley Cooper, Sir George Carteret, Sir William Berkeley, Sir George Colleton and William, Lord Craven.

Sir William Berkeley, on September 25, 1663, granted 2000 acres on the west side of the Pasquotank River to Mary Fortsen, the first woman to own land in North Carolina.

The Lords Proprietors established the first three counties in North Carolina: Albemarle, Clarendon and Craven.

An act established in 1666 stated: "every servant is to receive two suits of clothing and a set of tools" when his time of service was up.

A hurricane passed over the Outer Banks of Carolina on September 6, 1667. Rains from the storm lasted 12 days.

George Fox, founder of the Quakers, spent 18 days in the Albemarle region during November 1672.

Chowanos Indians attacked white settlers in the Albemarle region during 1675.

The estimated population of the Carolina Colony in 1675 was 4,000.

In 1677 the courts were given jurisdiction over "felonious witchcraft, sorceries, magic acts and fortune telling."

On December 2, 1689 Governor Seth Sothel was removed from office because of office misuse.

The first library in North Carolina opened in Bath in 1700 with books sent from England by Rev. Thomas Bray.

Baron Christoph de Graffenried of Switzerland founded New Bern in 1710.

The Society for Propagation of the Gospel endowed the first free school in North Carolina in the town of Bath.

The estimated population in the Colony during 1730 was 30,000 whites and 6,000 blacks (bond and free).

Hundreds of Waxhaw Indians died as a result of smallpox in 1740.

A 1750 hurricane on North Carolina's coast destroyed five ships.

Jared Irwin was born in Union County in 1750. In 1757 he moved to Georgia and was elected Governor of Georgia in 1796-98 and 1806-08.

Cherokee Indians surrounded Fort Dobbs on February 23, 1760 but were beaten back by Hugh Waddell.

Tryon's Palace in New Bern was completed in 1770. It was described as the "finest government house in English America."

On September 24-25, 1770 a mob of 150 Regulators, armed with sticks and switches, broke into the courtroom at Hillsborough and drove the judge outside.

The Assembly passed a law on April 1, 1780: any person who shall steal or shall by violence, seduction or any other means take away a slave, bond or free, shall suffer death without benefit of the clergy.

The first official census of the United States in 1790 tabulated North Carolina's population at 393,751: 288,204 whites; 100,572 slaves; and 4,975 free blacks.

President George Washington appointed John Skinner of Perquimans County as first Federal Marshall for North Carolina in 1790.

On February 13, 1800 citizens at Fort Johnston in Brunswick County held a memorial service to honor George Washington who died on December 14, 1799.

A riot occurred on June 28, 1810 between the pilots of Smithville (Southport) and the sailors of some European ships; many arrests occurred as a result of this incident.

During 1820 the first Roman Catholic priest arrived at St. Paul's church in New Bern.

The Baptist State Convention was established in Pitt County on March 26, 1830.

On March 7, 1840 the last spike in the Wilmington-Weldon Railroad was put into place, making it the longest railroad in the world at that time (161½ miles).

In 1850 President Millard Fillmore appointed as Secretary of the Navy William A Graham who had served as Governor from 1845-49.

The State Penitentiary opened in a log building in Raleigh on January 6, 1870.

Celia Busbee, a mentally-ill woman, tried to clean out her neighborhood on South Blount Street in Raleigh with an axe on January 20, 1880.

James B. Duke formed the American Tobacco Company in Durham on January 31, 1890.

From 1900 to 1907 Reginald A. Fessenden conducted successful experiments to transmit wireless (radio) messages from Roanoke Island and Cape Hatteras to Cape Henry, Virginia.

Thomas Sewell organized the first black YMCA Conference in the South at Bricks, Edgecombe County in 1920.

North Carolina's population in 1930 was 3,170,276 and represented an increase of 611,153 from 1920.

The United States Coast Guard station at Elizabeth City was dedicated on October 17, 1940.

North Carolina State College (later North Carolina State University) established the nation's first Nuclear Engineering course on June 12, 1950.

Henderson County had 200,000 productive apple trees with a cash crop value of $2,750,000 in 1960.

Thomas Rolfe, who settled on the Pasquotank River plantation in 1663, is believed to be the first physician in North Carolina.

In their concessions of 1665, the Lords Proprietors gave a Master (white settler) 51 acres of land for every slave 14 years or older imported into North Carolina.

On October 10, 1679 Virginia banned importation of Carolina tobacco because "the importation of trash tobacco greatly injuries the respected Virginia leaf."

In 1682, Joel Gascoyne of London published *A True Discription of Carolina*.

On February 25, 1695 Thomas Abington took oath as Attorney General of North Carolina. He served only until October 3, 1696.

John Lawson, surveyor, began his thousand-mile travel through North Carolina on December 28, 1700.

In 1701 the Reverend Daniel Brett became the first Anglican minister in the colony.

The first mention of Jews in North Carolina was made in 1702 when a formal protest was made that "Jews, strange sailors, servants, Negroes and others not qualified to vote have been allowed to cast ballots."

In 1712 Edward Mashbone conducted a school for whites and Indians at Sarum in Gates County.

The town of Beaufort was laid out in 1715 and named for Henry Somerset (1684-1714), Duke of Beaufort and one of the Lords Proprietors. Beaufort was incorporated in 1723.

In 1733 the ship *Marget,* bound from Charleston to London, wrecked offshore of Bodie Island; 11 people perished in the tragedy.

The town of Brunswick was thriving in 1731, with over 42 ships loaded with exports sailing during the year.

In 1741 Spanish privateers commandeered Ocracoke Island, seized incoming vessels and invaded the town.

James Davis of New Bern printed the first newspaper in the colony, *The North Carolina Gazette*, on August 9, 1751.

Colonel James Grant's troops, aided by Chickasaw and Catawba Indians, defeated Cherokees near Franklin in western North Carolina on June 10, 1761.

Queens College in Charlotte was established on January 15, 1771.

Jesse Grimes was born in Duplin County on February 6, 1781 and moved to Texas in 1826. He was a great military leader in Texas and signed the Texas Declaration of Independence and Constitution on March 17, 1836.

Following the signing of the Constitution, President George Washington named Sara DeCrow of Hertford the first woman postmaster in the United States on September 27, 1792.

Falkener Seminary, the first boarding school for girls, opened in Warrenton in 1801.

Eng and Chang, the Siamese twins born in 1811, died in 1874 as citizens of North Carolina.

The statue of George Washington by Italian sculptor Antonia Conova was unveiled in the rotunda of the State House on December 24, 1821.

On September 11, 1960 Hurricane Donna crossed Florida twice, then entered North Carolina near Topsail Beach with wind gusts of 100 miles per hour.

In 1970 North Carolina had the largest highway system in the nation with 73,036 miles of highways.

North Carolina's population in 1970 was 5,082,059.

The first hurricane ever recorded on the North Carolina coast was in 1524, thus the "Cape of Fear" appeared in the annals of history.

In the summer of 1567 Captain Juan Pardo led a Spanish expedition into western North Carolina.

On August 17, 1585 Sir Walter Raleigh's first colony landed on Roanoke Island.

Indian Manteo was baptized and given the title of "Lord of Roanoke" on August 13, 1587.

On August 18, 1590 John White reached Roanoke Island and found no trace of the colony of 1587. This became known as "The Lost Colony."

A "great fire" at Fayetteville destroyed over 600 homes and businesses on May 29, 1831.

In 1831 the General Assembly made it unlawful to cut off a person's ear as punishment.

Edward Burlson was born in Buncombe County on December 15, 1793. He later moved to Texas and was elected Vice President of the Republic of Texas in 1841.

Millie-Christine McCoy, Siamese twins, were born to Jacob and Monemia, slaves in Columbus County, on July 11, 1851.

On January 27, 1871 S.S. *Kensington* and *Bark Templar* collide off Cape Hatteras; 150 lives were lost.

The first city hospital in the state opened in Wilmington on January 29, 1881.

The steamer *St. Catharis* wrecked off Rodanthe with a loss of 90 lives on April 16, 1891.

In 1901 the Main Building at Buie's Creek Academy (Campbell University) was destroyed by fire.

After February 20, 1901 the executions of capital crimes (by hanging) at the seat of the county where the crime was committed, thereafter were carried out in private.

The University of North Carolina gave an honorary degree to Governor Woodrow Wilson of New Jersey on May 30, 1911.

On January 31, 1921 the *Carroll A. Deering* ran aground on the North Carolina coast. The crew of the ship was never found.

In 1931 the General Assembly adopted the secret ballot system that was intended to reduce vote buying since the buyer would no longer be able to confirm the results of his buy-out.

On April 30, 1941 William C. Lee, a native of Dunn, was appointed first commander of the Parachute School created by the War Department.

John D. Rockefeller, Jr. donated Linville Gorge, located in Burke County, to the National Park Service on February 7, 1951.

Maria Beale Fletcher of Asheville was crowned Miss America on September 9, 1961.

On February 6, 1971 race relations flared in Wilmington when a white-owned grocery store was burned. Ten people were convicted for the burning.

Luis Vasques deAyllon claimed the land between the Cape Fear and the Santee Rivers for Spain on June 30, 1521.

In May 1540 Hernando de Soto crossed North Carolina in search of gold.

Sir Walter Raleigh brought smoking tobacco to England in 1601 where smoking became a popular pastime.

North Carolina was separated from South Carolina in 1712.

In 1712 three counties changed names: Archdale became Craven; Wickham became Hyde and Pamptecough became Beaufort.

In 1752 a hurricane completely destroyed the town of Johnston in Onslow County.

In December 1771 Joseph Pilmoor preached the first real Methodist sermon in North Carolina at the Currituck Court House.

The General Assembly passed the following law in 1741:

> *Any Negro, malatto, or Indian, bond or free,*
> *found to give false testimony, without further*
> *trial be made to have one ear nailed to the*
> *pillory and there stand for a period of one*
> *hour, and then the said ear to be cut off,*
> *and thereafter the other ear nailed in like*
> *manner, and cut off at the end of one hour,*
> *and moreover such offender be given 39 lashes*
> *against his or her bare back well laid on.*

John Elmsley, born in 1762 in Halifax, moved with his parents to England in 1768. In 1796 Elmsley was named Chief Justice of Upper Canada and became Chief Justice of Lower Canada in 1801.

A law passed by the General Assembly: Any persons who have left this state, gone over to the enemy and joined the same, his land and Negroes shall be sold. William Tryon and Josiah Martin, ex-governors, headed the list.

On April 5, 1792 Joel Lane of Wake County signed a deed to the state for 1,000 acres of land for which the city of Raleigh would be laid.

The General Assembly passed the following law on December 17, 1802: The Governor shall reside permanently in the City of Raleigh, during his term of office.

Paul Barringer of Cabarrus County was commissioned a Brigadier General during the War of 1812.

In 1822 the Fayetteville town council passed an ordinance: every household is permitted to let one breeding sow run at large, after a license has been secured.

Stewart Ellison, a slave in Beaufort County, was born on March 8, 1832. He came to Raleigh around 1852 and in 1869 became the first black elected to serve on the Raleigh City Council. He served on the council for 12 years.

The Leonard Medical School, established in Raleigh at Shaw University, later became a part of the medical school at the University of North Carolina.

Meredith College in Raleigh was chartered in 1891 but did not open until 1899.

The annual report from the governor's office reported that there were five lynchings in the state during 1892.

In the May 25, 1901 issue of the *Raleigh News and Observer*, an editorial stated that the "Duke cigarettes not only destroy the mind and body and home, but give this country a bad name abroad."

The Grove Park Inn in Asheville was completed in 1912, taking 11 months, using 700 men and 400 mules, 24 hours a day.

The Coast Guard Cutter *Icarus* sank the German U-boat *V-352* off Cape Lookout on May 9, 1942.

In 1922 while in Italy, Ruth Faison Shaw who operated the Shaw School for English Boys and Girls, discovered the art of finger painting. Shaw was born in Kenansville, Duplin County.

On May 14, 1932 the North Carolina Symphony performed for the first time at Hill Hall on the campus of the University of North Carolina.

The mile-high swinging bridge atop Grandfather Mountain opened to the public on September 2, 1952.

The first North Carolinian killed in the Vietnam War was Floyd Milton Frazier of Waynesville who died in February 1962.

On April 5, 1972 the first block of four stamps was issued on "first day" sale at Cape Hatteras in honor of the 100th Anniversary of the Cape Hatteras National Seashore.

The first meeting of Nursing was held in the Chowan Precinct on April 4, 1703.

During March 20-23, 1713 South Carolina again sent aid to North Carolina in its fight with the Tuscarora Indians. All the Indians captured were sold as slaves.

In 1733 Governor George Burrington notified England that North Carolina was ready to ship 50,000 fat hogs north.

A law passed by Council in 1741 said: "if any white man or woman intermarry with an Indian, Negro, mustee or malatto, by judgement of the court shall be fined 50 pounds."

A law enacted in 1835: no slave shall hunt with a dog or dogs without having a certificate. If found offending this act, any person shall kill or destroy said dog and slave shall be given 30 lashes, well laid on his bare back.

In February1763 a reservation was established for the Catawba Indians who numbered 4,600 in South Carolina at that time.

At a meeting of freeholders in Rowan County on August 8, 1774, a resolution was passed that stated that the African trade was injurious to the colony.

Fifty-five women met in the King home in Edenton on October 25, 1774 to protest the British tea tax. This gathering gained fame as the Edenton Tea Party.

In 1782 Hillsborough was named the State's capital. A year later, the action was repealed.

First Class postage in 1792 was as follows: less than 30 miles, six cents; 30-60 miles, eight cents; 60 to 100 miles, 10 cents; 100-150 miles, 12 ½ cents.

A slave uprising was discovered on June 2, 1802 in Bertie County. The plot was not carried out and 11 slaves were executed.

In 1812 the food at Fort Johnston in Brunswick County was so scarce that the troops were required to fish the Cape Fear River to supplement their daily diet.

The State's first Temperance Society was organized in Greensboro in 1822.

The General Assembly passed a law in 1842: A man convicted of bigamy shall be branded with a large "B" on his cheek.

The North Carolina Agricultural Society was formed on October 8, 1852.

The first registered Guernsey cattle arrived in North Carolina by way of Forsyth County in 1882.

In 1892 John Van Lindley who planted 50,000 trees, established the first large-scale peach farm in Moore County.

It was reported on March 22, 1922 that North Carolina's textile mills had 5,253,199 active spindles, second only to Massachusetts.

The first Greek College and Orphanage in the United States was dedicated in Gastonia on September 18, 1932.

A Japanese submarine blew an 18 x 32 foot hole in the battleship *North Carolina* on September 15, 1942.

On January 2, 1952 the temperature at the Raleigh-Durham Airport reached 79 degrees, making it the hottest day ever recorded in January.

In March 1962 Susie Sharp became the first woman to serve on a State Supreme Court. She later became Chief Justice.

On August 28, 1972 Captain Richard S. Richie, a native of Reidsville, became the first Air Force "Ace" during the Vietnam War.

Queen Elizabeth granted Sir Walter Raleigh a charter to explore the new world on March 25, 1584.

North Carolina issued its first paper money in 1713.

A report issued August 31, 1843 stated that 26 lives were lost to yellow fever in 35 days at Washington, North Carolina.

William Rufus King was born on April 7, 1786 in Sampson County and later moved to Alabama. After his election to the Vice Presidency, he went to Cuba for health reasons and was sworn in there. He returned to the United States and died on April 18, 1853.

The Central Institute was established in 1883 at Littleton. It became Littleton Female College in 1887 and was destroyed by fire in 1919.

In 1893 Rufus L. Patterson, Jr. of Salem invented the "Patterson Packer," a machine that automatically weighed, packed, stamped and labeled smoking tobacco.

On January 29, 1903 North Carolina became the first state to require examination and registration of trained nurses.

In 1913 the General Assembly enacted this law: no person under the age of 16 could work in a factory or manufacturing establishment between 9 PM and 6 AM.

Willis Richardson's play *The Chipwoman's Fortune* opened on Broadway on May 15, 1923. This was the first play produced by a black on Broadway; Richardson was born in Wilmington.

A train wreck near Lumberton on December 16, 1943 became the state's worst train accident. Seventy-two people perished in the tragedy.

The original ACC basketball league was formed on May 8, 1953 in Greensboro. The charter members were: University of North Carolina, Duke, Clemson, Maryland, Wake Forest, North Carolina State and South Carolina.

Tar was first produced in North Carolina in 1704.

In March 1714 most of the Tuscarora Indians in Eastern North Carolina moved to upstate New York.

The first tobacco market in North Carolina opened in 1734 at Bellair in Craven County.

On April 20, 1744 the General Assembly appointed a commission to construct Fort Johnston on the Cape Fear River near Brunswick Town; construction began in 1745.

Robert Palmer took the oath of office as Collector of the Port of Bath on November 8, 1753.

In 1754 the General Assembly banned "the slitting of noses, the biting or cutting off a nose or lip, and the biting or cutting off any limb or member" in the sport of gouging.

The first chartered school in North Carolina, the New Bern Academy, opened on January 1, 1764.

The General Assembly passed a law in 1842 stating: wood sold in this state shall be by the cord. A cord of wood shall measure eight feet in length, four feet in height and four feet in breadth.

The lighthouse on Bald Head Island at the mouth of the Cape Fear River was lit for the first time on December 14, 1794.

Moravians from Pennsylvania purchased a tract of land in Piedmont North Carolina on November 17, 1753. They called the land "Wachovia."

Governor Alexander Martin laid before the General Assembly on April 19, 1783, a copy of the Peace Treaty with England. He said, "This is the most important intelligence that has yet arrived on the American Continent."

The Fayetteville Independent Light Infantry Company was formed August 23, 1793.

The General Assembly rejected a plan for a military school in the state in 1802.

Michael Schinck established the first cotton mill in North Carolina near Lincolnton in 1813.

John Stark Ravenscroft became the first Bishop of the Protestant Episcopal Church in North Carolina on May 22, 1823.

The first railroad in North Carolina was established in January 1833. It was an experimental road laid one and one-half miles from the site of the new capitol to the rock quarry. All the railroad cars were horse-drawn.

The General Assembly conducted its first meeting in the new State House in Raleigh on December 30, 1794.

The first banks in North Carolina were the Bank of the Cape Fear in Wilmington and the Bank of New Bern; both opened for business in 1804.

John Lineback of Salem was given a patent for the first cottonseed-hulling machine in America on March 31, 1814.

On June 25, 1824 an ad appeared in the *Raleigh Star* offering a $10 reward for a runaway apprentice, Andrew Johnson, who became President of the United States in 1865.

The Wake Forest Institute opened in 1834. The school moved to Winston Salem in 1956 and gained university status in 1967.

Fire destroyed a large part of Wilmington on April 30, 1844.

Harley B. Ferguson was born in Waynesville on August 14, 1875. He graduated from the United States Military Academy in 1897 and became the Executive Officer in charge of raising the U.S.S. *Maine* in Havana, Cuba in 1910. He was promoted to Brigadier General in 1918 and retired from service in 1939.

The Chicamocomico Life Saving Station on the Outer Banks opened in 1874. In 1915 it became a part of the U.S. Coast Guard Station; the station was decommissioned in 1954.

On February 20, 1884 a cyclone caused heavy damage, loss of life and property losses in Richmond, Harnett, Anson and Cumberland counties; about 50 people were killed in Richmond County.

The state's first School of Nursing opened at Rex Hospital in Raleigh in 1894.

A category III hurricane passed near Cape Hatteras on the Outer Banks on November 13, 1904.

A law passed by the General Assembly on September 16, 1914: children with as much as one-sixteenth Negro blood may not attend school with white children.

Trinity College, located in Durham, changed its name to Duke University on December 29, 1924.

In 1924 Anna Forbes Liddell was the first woman to receive a doctor of philosophy degree at the University of North Carolina.

During the war, in 1944, soft metal was so scarce that old toothpaste containers had to be turned in before you could purchase a fresh container.

Hurricane Hazel made a direct hit on Brunswick County on October 15, 1954; it traveled up through Raleigh and northward into Canada. Nineteen were killed; 200 injured; 15,000 homes and structures destroyed; and $136 million in property damages were sustained.

On May 7, 1964 President L.B. Johnson, in pushing his "War on Poverty," visited a Rocky Mount tenant farmer, William Marlow.

The population in North Carolina in 1715 was estimated at 11,200; the total included 3,700 slaves.

A law enacted in 1715: before anyone in North Carolina could have a private funeral, three or four persons must be called to view the corpse. If it appears the corpse met a violent death, it must be reported. Also, all plantation owners shall set aside a burial place, and fence same for the burial of all persons – bond or free.

Brunswick Town on the lower Cape Fear River was established in 1725.

The first survey of North and South Carolina's border was conducted from May to October 1735.

On April 20, 1745 the first liquor-control law was adopted: Any person or tavern keeper who allows any person to get drunk in his house on the Sabbath, shall be fined 10 shillings.

James Davis of New Bern received a contract for the first postal service in the state in October 1755.

Five hundred men gathered in Wilmington on October 19, 1765 to demonstrate against the British Stamp Act that had been passed on March 22. On November 16, the Sons of Liberty marched from Wilmington to Brunswick and forced the Stamp Master to resign.

Five hundred minutemen under John Ashe and Cornelius Harnett burned down the building inside Fort Johnston at Brunswick Town on July 18, 1775. This was the first overt act of the War for Independence in this colony.

In 1978 the United States Department of Energy and the Blue Ridge Electric Corporation erected the world's largest windmill atop Howard's Knob at Boone. The cost was thirty million dollars. It was the world's first wind-driven megawatt electric generator. The system went into operation in 1981 and was torn down in 1983.

A tornado that killed four and injured 157, ripped through Raleigh in the early morning hours on November 28, 1989.

A snowfall that began at 8:30 PM on January 24, 2000 and ended at 2:30 PM the following day, accumulated 20.3 inches of snow in the triangle area of North Carolina —a record. School children in Wake County were out of school for seven days.

On September 5, 1979 Hurricane David moved through Florida and South Carolina before entering North Carolina and leaving extensive damage.

On June 8, 1999 the citizens of Wake County rejected a $650-million school bond, with 65.3% voting against and 34.7% in favor. This was the largest school bond proposal in the history of the state.

According to the 1980 census, North Carolina's population reached 5,881,385.

At a news conference in Durham, city officials dropped the city's slogan "Bull City" in favor of "The City of Medicine."

President Bill Clinton addressed the North Carolina General Assembly on March 13, 1997. He was the first president to address the Assembly.

The coldest temperature ever recorded on Grandfather Mountain reached 27 degrees below zero on January 11, 1982.

On September 5, 1996 Hurricane Fran made a direct hit on North Carolina. Thirty-four lives were lost, and more than 1,000,000 citizens were without electric power for several days.

Deneen Zezell Graham of North Wilkesboro became North Carolina's first black Miss North Carolina on June 25, 1983.

On April 4, 1983 the North Carolina State University basketball team defeated the University of Houston 54 to 52 for the NCAA National Basketball Championship.

Hurricane Bertha, which hit North Carolina's coast and eastern section on July 12, 1996, destroyed a fishing pier and several houses. Because the storm hit during the busy summer season on the coast, $6,000,000 in business was lost per day. The storm also caused over $200,000,000 in crop damage.

The first person to be executed by lethal injection in North Carolina was James Hutchins who was executed on March 16, 1984.

A cigarette butt in a trash bag ignited and destroyed the Phi Gamma Delta fraternity house in Chapel Hill, killing five people on May 11, 1996.

On April 22, 1985 doctors at Duke Medical Center performed the first successful heart transplant in the state.

During the 1985 session of the General Assembly, that body enacted the state's first seat belt law under which a citizen was fined $25 if caught not wearing his belt.

On January 6 and 7 in 1996, the "Blizzard of '96" dumped 28 inches of snow in the mountains, over eight inches in the Piedmont and more than five inches in the Triangle in a 24-hour period. Eight people were killed as a result of the storm.

The "First Lady in Song" Kate Smith died in Raleigh on June 17, 1986. Miss Smith had been living in Raleigh for several years.

During the 1995 session of the state legislature, the sweet potato was adopted as the state vegetable.

On September 5, 1987, overzealous students from East Carolina University ransacked Carter-Finley Stadium following ECU's victory over North Carolina State University 32-14.

A DC-9 U.S. Air flight crashed near Charlotte, killing 37 and injuring 20 on July 2, 1994.

On February 1, 1988 two Indians with guns took over a Lumberton newspaper office, holding employees hostage for 10 hours.

Maya Angelou, professor of American Studies at Wake Forest University, delivered her poem "A Rock, A River, A Tree" at the inauguration of president-elect William Jefferson Clinton on January 20, 1993.

Hurricane Hugo made landfall at Charleston, South Carolina on September 21, 1989, then entered North Carolina near Charlotte on the 22nd, causing one billion dollars in damage and leaving 500,000 people without electricity.

In special ceremonies, the new Coast Guard Station on Oak Island opened in March 1992.

The 1990 census showed that North Carolina's population had grown to 6,628,637.

On September 3, 1991 a fire at the Imperial Food Plant in Hamlet left 25 dead and 55 injured.

In the June 5, 1990 primary, Democratic candidate Harvey Gant won his party's nomination for the U.S. Senate. Gant was the first black in state history to be a candidate for this office. In the November general election, Republican candidate Jesse Helms defeated Gant.

The Communist Worker Party and the KKK clashed in Greensboro on November 3, 1979, resulting in the death of five members of the Communist party.

On November 7, 2000 Democratic candidate Mike Easley won the election for Governor and Democratic candidate Beverly Purdue won the seat for Lt. Governor. Purdue was the first woman to hold that office. Both were sworn into office in January 2001.

Hurricane Floyd brought record flooding to eastern North Carolina and caused 51 deaths on September 15, 1999.

The Washington Redskins named Joe Gibbs, a native of Mocksville, as head football coach on January 13, 1981. Gibbs won three Super Bowls with the Redskins.

On April 25, 1997 United States District Judge William L. Osteen ruled in Greensboro that the Food and Drug Administration could regulate sales and labeling of cigarettes, but that it has no authority over advertising.

President Clinton visited Raleigh on September 14, 1996 to view the aftermath of Hurricane Fran.

On June 19, 1996 the season's first tropical storm Arthur brushed North Carolina's coastal area and caused heavy flooding. Another severe storm followed Arthur on the 25th and spawned tornadoes, damaged the coastal area, and injured 19 Marines from Camp Lejeune by lightning strikes.

During special activities in 1984, the *Elizabeth II* replica of the 1585 ship that brought English colonists to Roanoke Island was christened at Manteo.

Two-dozen tornadoes ripped through North and South Carolina on March 28, 1984 causing 69 deaths, injuring over 1,300 and leaving 3,100 homeless.

On May 10, 1996 a Boeing CH46 SeaKnight and an AH-1 Cobra Helicopter collided in mid-air during Camp Lejeune exercises and killed 14 persons.

During the General Assembly session of 1985, the legal drinking age was raised from 18 to 19 years of age.

The winter storm of February 2-5, 1996 brought an extra heavy snowfall over the state leaving 19 people dead and over 350,000 without power; the temperature fell to minus 13 degrees.

Hurricane Charley crossed the Outer banks of North Carolina on August 18, 1986.

On June 13, 1995 Mother Teresa, winner of the Nobel Peace Prize, visited Charlotte.

The Martin Luther King, Jr. holiday was adopted by the North Carolina General Assembly in 1987. In the same session, legislators adopted milk as the state's official beverage and the shad boat as the state's historical boat.

In a 1994 report, the average cost system-wide for housing inmates in the North Carolina prison system was $58.58 per day, per inmate.

On September 25, 1988 presidential candidates George Bush and Michael Dukakis held the first of two national debates at Wake Forest University.

North Carolina State University's beloved basketball coach Jim Valvano died at the Duke Medical Center on April 28, 1993. Valvano's 1983 team won the national basketball championship despite great odds. Shortly before his death, he encouraged the students at N.C. State and everywhere to "Never give up!"

The nationally televised basketball game between the University of North Carolina and North Carolina State University on January 16, 1991 was postponed when the news reached the schools that the Persian Gulf War had started.

The state budget woes were so severe on May 4, 1990 that the state announced that it was delaying $51.7 million in income tax refunds.

On July 18, 1990 Vice President Dan Quayle visited Raleigh.

The estimated population of the Carolina Colony in 1675 was 4,000.

A town was laid out at Forks of Queen Anne Creek in 1715. Later the town's name was changed to Edenton.

The home of Roger Moore was built just north of Brunswick Town and called Orton Plantation in 1725.

A survey completed in 1735 established the boundary line between North and South Carolina.

James Davis of New Bern, the state printer, was awarded the first contract for postal service in North Carolina in 1755.

Fire destroyed the Bladen County Courthouse and all its records in 1765.

The last court under royal rule was held in the home of Colonel Joel Lane in Wake County on March 5, 1775.

John Jones McRae, born on January 10, 1815 in Anson County, moved to Mississippi in 1818. In 1854 he was elected Governor of that state.

President John Q. Adams appointed ex-governor William Miller of Warren County Diplomatic Agent to Guatemala in March 1825.

In 1835 the Baptist State Convention established the *Biblical Recorder*, the official newspaper of the denomination.

Fifty-three buildings were destroyed by fire in Fayetteville on June 6, 1845.

In 1855 there were 17 crimes that carried the death penalty in North Carolina.

Henrey Wolff Butner was born on April 6, 1875 in Pinnacle, Stokes County. He graduated from West Point and obtained the rank of Major General. Camp Butner in Person County was named in his honor.

President Grover Cleveland appointed former governor Thomas J. Jarvis as the ambassador to Brazil in July 1885.

On May 20, 1895 Julia Jackson Christian, Granddaughter of General Stonewall Jackson, unveiled the Confederate monument on Union Square in Raleigh.

Anna Morrison Jackson, the widow of General Stonewall Jackson, died on March 24, 1915 in Charlotte where she made her home.

Kathryn Rachel Sarah Rebecca Speight Darden Davis was born on September 24, 1905 in Seven Springs, Wayne County. She became an outstanding physician and served in the North Carolina Legislature from 1959-1963.

An explosion killed 60 miners at Glen Coal Mine near Sanford on May 27, 1925.

On February 18, 1979 the weather bureau at Raleigh-Durham International Airport reported a snowfall measuring 10.4 inches.

During the 1979 session of the General Assembly, the box turtle was named the official state reptile and the granite stone was named the official state rock.

Movers began the arduous task of moving Cape Hatteras Lighthouse 2900 feet from the sea on June 17, 1999. Although the move was completed in 23 days, the famous light was not turned on again until November 13th.

On March 1-2, 1980 the Triangle area was hit with an 11.1-inch blanket of snow.

Dean Smith announced his retirement as head coach of the University of North Carolina men's basketball team on March 15, 1997.

On June 6, 1997 *The Lost Colony* began its 60th season with performance number 3,269.

In 1982 the School of Veterinary Medicine enrolled its first class at North Carolina State University.

On September 4, 1996 torrential rains flooded the mountains, causing Lake Lure to flood and washing away roads, homes and businesses.

The highest temperature recorded in North Carolina history was on August 23, 1983 when the thermometer hit 110 degrees at Fayetteville.

On June 13, 1996 the Freeman standoff of 81 days in Montana was concluded with the arrest of 14 people, some of whom were natives of Johnston County.

Republican Jesse Helms won his third six-year term in the United States Senate on November 6, 1984. He defeated the Democratic candidate James B. Hunt, Jr.

Tornadoes swept through Zebulon, Wendell and Pilot on April 15, 1996, leaving 31 people injured and 36 homes destroyed.

Hurricane Gloria swept across the Outer Banks near Cape Hatteras on September 27, 1985.

On March 12, 1996 Secretary of State Rufus Edmondson resigned his office effective March 31. On April 1, Janice Faulkner took the oath of office, replacing Edmondson.

During the 1995-96-winter season in the mountains of North Carolina, there was a total of 116 inches of snow.

Gertrude Elion and George Hitchings of Burroughs Welcome in the Research Triangle won the Nobel Prize for Medicine on October 17, 1988.

An announcement on April 23, 1990 declared that North Carolina ranked last in the United States in per capita expenditures for state parks.

On June 29, 1990 the final segment of Interstate 40 opened at Newton Grove in Sampson County.

Pat Crawford, a member of the famous "Gashouse Gang" of the 1934 World Champion St. Louis Cardinals, died in a Morehead City hospital on January 25, 1994.

Comedienne Martha Raye was laid to rest on October 22, 1994 at the military burial ground at Fort Bragg. She is the only civilian to be buried there.

On December 13, 1994 a commuter plane trying to land at the Raleigh-Durham International Airport crashed, killing 15 people.

Ava Gardner, born in Johnston County and one of the most beautiful stars of Hollywood, was laid to rest in the family plot at Smithfield on January 25, 1990.

On March 6, 1990 the General Assembly held an emergency session to discuss the state's overcrowded prisons.

The state's longest trial (eight months) ended on August 19, 1991 when Fred F. Kelly, Jr. was found guilty on 99 charges of sexual abuse in Edenton.

On October 26, 1993 the National Football League awarded Charlotte an expansion franchise, the Carolina Panthers.

According to the 1860 census, the population of North Carolina was 992,622.

Thomas O. Moore, born in Sampson County on April 10, 1804, was inaugurated Governor of Louisiana on January 23, 1860.

Edward Austin Johnson, born a slave in Wake County on November 23, 1806, authored *A School History of the Negro Race in America*. It was the first textbook on this subject that was approved for public school instruction in North Carolina.

Sampson Lane Faison was born in Faison, Duplin County on November 29, 1860. Faison served in the United States Army in World War I and on June 14, 1922 was promoted to Brigadier General. As Acting Major General on September 29, 1918, Faison and his 60th Infantry Brigade were the first Americans to break through the "impenetrable" Hindenburg Line at Belocourt, France.

It was reported by the 1860 census that 97.5 percent of the North Carolina population was classified as "rural."

Joseph Roswell Hawley was born in Richmond County. He was a follower of Abraham Lincoln and in 1861 became the first North Carolinian to join the Union Army.

An official report issued on January 5, 1861 showed that 6,775,286 pounds of rice and 100,000 bushels of corn were produced in Brunswick County during the previous year.

Charles A. Smith, born in Hertford, North Carolina, was elected Lt. Governor of South Carolina on January 22, 1861. When Governor Cole Blease resigned, Smith served as governor the five days preceding South Carolina's secession from the Union.

At Ansonville, North Carolina two young men fashioned a calico flag to serve as an incentive to get the local citizens to encourage the state to leave the union. When the flag was raised on February 1, 1861, the citizens of the town cut it down.

The Chatham Railroad was chartered on February 15, 1861.

Willie P. Mangum, Jr., a native of Wake County, was commissioned as Consul to Ning-po, China on March 27, 1861. In 1865 he was appointed Consul to Nagasaki, Japan, and he established the first American mail service to China in 1867.

Chapter 2
The Civil War in
North Carolina

A CHRONOLOGY OF EVENTS AND SPECIAL HONORS BESTOWED ON NORTH CAROLINA SOLDIERS

1861

On January 9 citizens of Smithville (Southport) and Wilmington occupied Fort Johnston on the Cape Fear River.

Braxton Bragg, born in Warrenton on March 22, 1817, was appointed a Brigadier General in February.

In April a hurricane passed the coast of North Carolina, delaying and destroying several ships of the Union fleet as they prepared to blockade the coast.

Some 15 to 20 free blacks volunteered their service to the Confederate States at New Bern in April. They were the first blacks to offer service to the Confederacy.

On April 15 President Abraham Lincoln called on North Carolina to raise 75,000 troops to suppress the "Southern Insurrection."

Governor John Ellis, on April 15, ordered Captain M.D. Croton and his "Goldsborough Rifles" to occupy Fort Macon on the coast.

The Wilmington Light Infantry overtook Fort Caswell on the lower Cape Fear River on April 15. On the 16th, state troops took Fort Johnston at Brunswick Town.

President Abraham Lincoln issued an order to blockade all southern ports on April 19.

On April 20 the Charlotte Greys seized the United States Mint in Charlotte.

The commanding captain of the Federal Arsenal at Fayetteville surrendered to state troops on April 22.

On May 1 the North Carolina Legislature voted in favor of a state convention to consider secession.

The state convention met in Raleigh on May and voted to remove themselves from the Union and join the Confederate States of America.

Edmund Burke Haywood was appointed surgeon of the North Carolina state troops on May 16. He set up the first military hospital in the state during the War Between the States.

Governor Ellis appointed Dr. Charles E. Johnson of Raleigh as surgeon general of the North Carolina troops.

On May 17 President Jefferson Davis signed a bill admitting North Carolina to the Confederacy, contingent upon approval of the ordinance of secession and ratification of the Confederate Constitution. (North Carolina had not voted secession until May 20th).

Walter Gwynn, a native of West Virginia, accepted a commission as Brigadier General in the North Carolina Volunteers on May 25.

On June 27 arrangements were made for transfer of the state's military and naval forces to the Confederacy.

Upon the death of Governor John Ellis on July 7, the Speaker of the State Senate Henry T. Clark assumed the role of governor. Clark served until Zebulon B. Vance replaced him on September 8, 1862.

The United States Senate expelled the senators from North Carolina on July 11. This was a mere formality since the senators had already left Washington.

The *USS Daylight* established the first blockade of Wilmington July 14.

The steamer *Beaufort* was commissioned into Confederate service in July. She saw her first action on July 21 off Oregon Inlet.

The Federal side-wheel steamer *Harriet Lane* fired three salvos on Fort Clark in July; these were the first hostile shots against North Carolina.

Lt. R.C. Duval, commander of the North Carolina vessel *Beaufort*, reported the first naval engagement between Confederate and Union forces off the coast of North Carolina. Duval claimed victory on July 21.

The steamer *Raleigh* was fitted out and placed into Confederate service on July 22 under command of Lt. J.W. Alexander, CSN.

An old abandoned cotton mill at Salisbury was converted to use as a Confederate prison on July 30.

The *USS Union* chased the Confederate privateer *York* aground off Cape Hatteras on August 9.

James Wallace Cooke, born in Beaufort on August 13, 1812, resigned his US. Navy position and joined the Confederate navy in 1861. He later commanded the ironclad *CSS Albemarle* that was destroyed on October 27, 1864.

Richard Caswell Gatlin, born in Kinston on January 18, 1809, was noted as a brigadier general on August 16.

On August 26 Union army and navy transports (eight ships and 900 men) left Hampton Roads, Virginia for an assault on the forts along the North Carolina coast.

On August 27 Union forces attacked Fort Clark and Fort Hatteras. Both forts fell into Union hands on August 29th.

On August 27, Henry King Burgwyn, Jr. was promoted to the rank of Lt. Colonel. At age 19, he was the youngest colonel in the Confederate army.

On September 17 fighting took place at Ocracoke Inlet. This episode closed the Sound to any blockade-runners.

Confederate forces captured its first Union ship, the *USS Fanny*, on North Carolina's coast.

Confederate forces attacked an Indiana regiment at Chicamocomico near Hatteras Inlet on October 4.

The *Winslow*, the first ship commissioned in the North Carolina navy, was sunk at Ocracoke Inlet in November.

On November 22 President Jefferson Davis appointed former governor Thomas Bragg of Warrenton as Attorney General of the Confederate States of America. Bragg served until March 18, 1862.

On December 25 the *USS Fernandina* captured the Confederate schooner *William H. Northrup* off Cape Fear.

1862

The Federal Department of North Carolina was instituted on January 7 with General Ambrose Burnside in command.

On January 25, 1862 at Hatteras Inlet, the Burnside expedition moved transports and naval war vessels over the shallow bar into Pamlico Sound despite extreme difficulties.

After being removed from Portsmouth, Virginia, the Confederate Navy Yard was established in Charlotte.

General Burnside's Federal forces landed on Roanoke Island on February 7 after having encountered great difficulty moving vessels over the shallow bar at Hatteras Inlet. The Union gunboat *Underwriter* fired the first shot on the attack of Roanoke Island.

Union forces, under the command of General Ambrose Burnside, captured Roanoke Island on February 8 and took 2,000 prisoners.

The *Mosquito* fleet was destroyed on February 10 when Federals fought a successful engagement at Elizabeth City. This victory gave General Burnside firm control of coastal Carolina. He was prepared to move on to New Bern.

Federal naval forces captured the town of Edenton on February 12.

On February 13 a Federal expedition left North River for skirmish and control of Albemarle Canal.

The North Carolina General Assembly authorized the Governor to raise three batteries of artillery "to serve at the batteries already erected on the Cape Fear River."

Reports reached Raleigh on February 18 that Federal forces were operating around Winton, North Carolina.

Union troops destroyed the Hertford County Courthouse and all its records when they set torch to the building on February 20.

Union forces destroyed the town of Winton in Hertford County on February 20. This was the first town in North Carolina to be destroyed by fire during the war.

Under the cover of the Navy, Federal troops led by General Burnside landed on the west bank of the Neuse River, south of New Bern, and advanced upon the city on March 13.

On March 14 General Burnside with 11,000 men captured the town of New Bern, driving back about 4,000 Confederates under the command of General Lawrence O'Bryan Branch. Casualties for the Federals were 471, including 90 deaths. Confederate losses were placed at 600 with the majority captured or missing and 64 killed.

William Henry Forny, a native of Lincolnton, was promoted to Brigadier General on March 14. He was named a Major General on October 27.

On March 20, 1862 Burnside's Federal forces advanced to Washington, North Carolina.

The 1st Battalion of the North Carolina Light Artillery was mustered into service at Camp Mangum near Raleigh on March 28.

General Burnside ordered Brigadier General John G. Parke to move against Fort Macon on the coast on March 23. Upon arriving, Parke ordered the fort to surrender but it refused. The Federals then attacked the fort.

Lewis Addison Armistead, born in New Bern on February 18, 1817, was commissioned a Brigadier General in the Confederate service on April 1.

On April 7 there were several skirmishes at Foy's plantation and near Newport.

Action occurred at Gillett's farm on Pebbly Run on April 13.

On April 19 there were skirmishes between Federal and Confederate troops on Trent Road near New Bern.

Federal naval forces successfully blocked Chesapeake and Albemarle canals, shutting off an important small-boat waterway.

On April 26 Fort Macon formally surrendered, and the Confederate garrison of 400 became prisoners of Federal forces.

Fighting occurred on April 27 at Haughton's Mill near Pollocksville. Two days later the Federals attacked Confederates at Batchelder's Creek.

On May 2, Edward Stanly was appointed Federal military governor of North Carolina.

Federals continued several expeditions from Roanoke Island to Gatesville on May 7-8.

President Abraham Lincoln proclaimed the port of Beaufort open to commerce on May 12.

On May 15 Federal forces continued their assault on Trenton Bridge at Young's Crossroads and on areas near Pollocksville.

James G. Martin, a native of Elizabeth City, was promoted to Brigadier General on May 17, 1862.

On May 19 the 10th Battalion North Carolina Heavy Artillery was organized and mustered in Wilmington.

There was fighting at Pollocksville Crossroads and Trenton on May 22. Federal forces scouted in and around Tranter's Creek on May 30.

George B. Anderson, born near Hillsborough on April 12, 1831, graduated 9th in his class of 41 at West Point. Due to his bravery and courage in the battle of Fair Oaks on May 31, President Jefferson Davis promoted him to Brigadier General.

On July 4 Colonel William Lamb, a native of Virginia, assumed command of Fort Fisher located at the mouth of the Cape Fear River. Lamb served as commander of the fort until its surrender on January 15, 1865.

Federal forces captured the town of Hamilton on July 9.

Confederate general Daniel Harvey Hill was assigned to command the Department of North Carolina on July 17.

Reconnaissance and action occurred from Newport to Swansborough (Swansboro) on August 14.

Thomas Lanier Clingman, born in Surry County on July 27, 1812, was promoted to Brigadier General in August 1862. On August 18th he was assigned command at Wilmington.

There was a minor skirmish near Plymouth by Federals and Rebels on August 30.

Junius Daniel, a native of Halifax County, was commissioned Brigadier General on September 1.

Federal forces began their fierce attack on Washington on September 6.

Lawrence O'Bryan Branch, born in Enfield, served as Brigadier General during the Civil War. He was killed in the battle of Antietam on September 7.

On September 8 Colonel Zebulon B. Vance left New Bern to assume the governorship of the state.

On September 10 there was a terrifying outbreak of yellow fever in Wilmington.

Confederate and Union forces engaged in combat in and around Shiloh, Camden County on September 17.

In the battle of Antietam on September 17, the North Carolina 27th regiment lost 203 of its 325 men. Colonel John Rogers Cooke commanded the 27th regiment.

On October 1 the Confederate steamer *Raleigh* engaged the Federal steamer *Fanny*, loaded with ammunition and supplies. After a 55-minute battle, the *Fanny* surrendered. This was North Carolina's first successful naval engagement.

Annie Carter Lee, daughter of General Robert E. Lee, died in Warren County on October 20. She was buried in the county for fear that her body would be taken by Union forces on their way to Richmond.

On November 1 John Rogers Cooke was appointed Brigadier General.

On November 1 Stephen Douglas Ramseur was promoted to Brigadier General. Ramseur was born on May 13, 1837 in Lincolnton.

James Henry Lane, a former teacher of natural philosophy and tactics at the North Carolina Military Institute in Charlotte, was promoted to Brigadier General on November 1. When promoted, he was only 29 years old and was dubbed the "Little General."

Hertford County native Richard Gatling patented a revolving, 6-barrel gun known as the "Gatling Gun" on November 4.

Evander McNair, born in Richmond County on April 12, 1820, was promoted to Brigadier General following the battle of Richmond on November 4.

Five thousand Confederate soldiers died in the battle of Fredericksburg on December 13; more than one-third of the dead were from North Carolina.

The Confederate War Department commissioned Brigadier General Lucius Eugene Polk, a native of Salisbury.

On December 30 the Union ironclad *Monitor* sank in a gale off Cape Hatteras.

1863

Dr. A.S. Piggott established a medical laboratory in Lincoln County to produce medicines for the Confederacy.

In the Spring of 1863, the Shelton Laurel Massacre occurred; 13 men and boys suspected of Union sympathies were killed by Confederate soldiers in Madison County.

Samuel F. Patterson of Caldwell County was made Brigadier General of the State Militia. Before the end of the war, he was promoted to Major General.

James City in Craven County was founded as a camp for freed slaves. The town was named for Horace James, former Union Chaplin who supervised a freemen's camp on the site in 1865.

On January 1 President Lincoln's Emancipation Proclamation went into effect.

On January 13 the USS *Columbia* ran aground off the North Carolina coast. It was seized by Confederate forces and burned.

Federal troops conducted skirmishes and reconnaissance from January 17-21 at Trenton, Young's Crossroads, Onslow, Jacksonville and Northeast River.

Federal troops conducted reconnaissance on Neuse, Dover and Trent roads on January 27.

A Federal expedition from New Bern to Plymouth was carried out on February 1 and lasted for ten days.

On February 2 Federal forces destroyed some salt works at Wale's head in Currituck County.

There was a skirmish between Union and Confederate forces at Edenton on February 7. On February 10th, the forces opposed each other again at Batchelder's Creek.

On February 13, Union forces raided Washington and Sandy Ridge.

The three batteries that organized on February 15 were reorganized as the First Battalion, North Carolina Heavy Artillery.

Union forces fired on Fort Caswell on February 23.

General Longstreet assumed command of the Confederate Department of North Carolina and Virginia on February 26.

Several skirmishes marked a Federal expedition from New Bern to Swan Quarter from March 1-6.

On March 6, there were forays by Federals from New Bern to Trenton and Swansboro. There were also demonstrations at Kinston.

On March 7 Federals conducted reconnaissance from Newport barracks to Cedar Point. In addition, there was an expedition from New Bern to Mattamuskeet Lake.

At Salisbury, 200 women with hatchets defeated soldiers and successfully demanded flour from local merchants on March 15.

On March 15 the British *Britannia* successfully ran the blockade into Wilmington.

On March 30 Confederates laid siege to the city of Washington with skirmishes at Rodman's Point on the Pamlico River and near Deep Gully. Fighting continued until April 4 at which time Federal forces failed to capture a strong Confederate battery at Rodman's Point near Washington.

Federals left Washington on April 6 and raided the town of Nixonton in Pasquotank County.

Federal expeditions were carried out from New Bern to Swift Creek Village on April 13 and lasted until April 21.

On April 15 Confederate troops withdrew from their siege of Washington.

For 21 days starting on April 16, Federal expeditions were carried out from New Bern toward Kinston, including skirmishes at Core Creek, Big Swift Creek and Sandy Ridge.

Citizens of Wilmington cheered as four vessels that evaded the blockade entered the port city on April 23.

Wise Crossroads in Jones County saw action on April 27.

Robert Ranson, Jr., born in Warren County in 1828, was promoted to Major General in May.

On May 2 at Chancellorsville, the men from the 18th North Carolina Regiment had the misfortune of firing upon General Stonewall Jackson, resulting in his death on May 10th.

May 5 opened with a skirmish at Peletier's Mill in Carteret County.

There was demonstration at Kinston from May 20-23 and skirmishes at Gum Swamp and Batchelder's Creek.

A blockade-runner loaded with goods was captured on May 20 off the Neuse River in Craven County.

On May 27 William Dorsey Pender, who was born in Edgecombe County, was promoted to Major General. He was only 29 years old at the time.

On June 9 Benjamin Franklin Dixon of Cleveland County was commissioned a Captain in the Confederate Army. At age 17, he was one of the youngest captains in the Confederate service.

On June 12 Lt. Charles Read, daring commander of the *CSS Clarence*, captured the Union bark *Tacony* off Cape Hatteras.

Isham Warren Garrott, born in Wake County, moved to Alabama before the Civil War. On June 17 a Union sharpshooter killed Garrott. He had been promoted to Brigadier General on May 28 but the commission never reached him.

On June 17 Union forces scouted from Rocky Run to Dover and Core Creek in eastern North Carolina.

Of the 15, 301 Confederate soldiers were killed in the three-day battle of Gettysburg (July 1-3, 1863); 4033 were from North Carolina.

On July 3 Federal troops raided along the Wilmington and Weldon Railroad.

The Federal Cavalry destroyed the Confederate Arms Factory at Kenansville in Duplin County on July 4.

Following the destruction of the arms factory at Kenansville, the Union forces moved on to Warsaw and Magnolia on July 5.

Fighting broke out on July 6 at Free Bridge near Trenton, and Federals continued their raid on the Wilmington and Weldon Railroad.

On July 11 Daniel Harvey Hill was promoted to Lt. General. In the battle of Bentonville on March 19-21, 1865, Hill commanded as a Major General.

Federals continued their mop-up in eastern North Carolina with expeditions on July 13 at Newport Barracks, Cedar Point and Oak River.

On July 14 Major General W.H.C. Whiting was named commander of the Department of North Carolina.

Federal scouts moved from New Bern to Tarborough and Rocky Mount on July 18.

On July 20 the USS *Shawsheen* captured five schooners on the Neuse River near Cedar Island.

On July 21-22 there were Union expeditions from New Bern to Tarborough. There were also skirmishes at Street's Ferry and Scupperton.

Additional Union forces entered North Carolina from Portsmouth, Virginia and advanced toward Jackson, North Carolina on July 25. These troops moved toward Plymouth and Foster's Mill on the 26th.

In August President Jefferson Davis issued a proclamation of amnesty for all Confederate deserters.

Thomas Pleasant Dockery, born in Montgomery County, North Carolina, was promoted to the rank of Brigadier General on August 10.

A Federal expedition moved toward Edenton on August 11. At Washington, a large pro-Union meeting was held in support of the Federal war effort.

On August 31 William W. Kirkland was promoted to Brigadier General. Kirkland was born in Hillsborough, North Carolina.

Robert Daniel Johnston was promoted to Brigadier General on September 1. He was the youngest brigadier general in the Confederate service at age 26. He was a native of Lincoln County.

On September 3 a Georgia regiment moving through Raleigh destroyed the newspaper office of Union sympathizer William W. Holden.

On September 15, there was a Federal expedition from Great Bridge, Virginia to Indiantown in Camden County.

On September 28 Generals Robert E. Lee and J.E.B. Stuart recommended James B. Gordon for promotion to Brigadier General as a result of his heroic action during the Civil War. Gordon was born in Wilkesboro, North Carolina on November 2, 1822.

During 1863, the noted Confederate Ram *Albemarle* was built in Halifax County, North Carolina.

General Cooke's Regiment of North Carolinians lost 700 of its 1,400 men in 30 minutes in the Battle of Bristol Station, Virginia on October 24.

On November 23 President Jefferson Davis visited Fort Fisher on the coast of North Carolina.

Robert V. Richardson was appointed Brigadier General in the Confederate Army. Richardson was born in Granville County but moved to Tennessee at an early age.

On December 29 Daniel C. Govan was promoted to Brigadier General in the Confederate service. Govan was born in New Bern on July 4, 1829 and died on March 12, 1911.

1864

During 1864 the Confederates established a hospital and cemetery at Kittrell. There are 52 Confederate soldiers buried there.

A fire on Wilmington's waterfront in 1864 destroyed a large amount of naval stores.

Fire and an explosion of unknown cause on January 7 destroyed the Confederate Navy Yard at Charlotte.

Alexander M. Gorman purchased the *State Journal* newspaper on January 26 and converted it to the *Daily Confederate*, devoting it to the Confederate cause.

On February 1 Confederate troops under General Pickett moved from Kinston toward New Bern in an effort to recapture the important Federal base there.

Confederate navy men in small boats captured the U.S. gunboat *Underwriter* in the Neuse River near New Bern on February 2 but were forced to set it afire and flee.

Fighting occurred near Beaufort at Gale's Creek, Bogue Sound Blockhouse and Newport Barracks on February 2.

There was a Union reconnaissance toward Swansborough on February 8.

On February 10 the USS *Florida* destroyed two blockade-runners off Masonborough Inlet.

A Union expedition moved from Motley's Ford, Tennessee to Murphy in western North Carolina on February 17.

On March 4 Fabius Haywood Busbee of Raleigh joined the Confederate army at the age of 16. He held the rank of Second Lieutenant and was the youngest commissioned officer in the Confederate army.

On March 25   Federal troops conducted scouting operations from Beaufort to Bogue and Bear Inlets on the North Carolina coast.

Skirmishes broke out on April 1 at Plymouth.

Confederate forces destroyed the Cape Lookout Lighthouse light on April 2.

General P.G.T. Beauregard was ordered to Weldon on April 15 to head off any Union troops in the area.

Confederate land forces, soon to be joined by the nearly finished ram *Albemarle*, began an attack on Plymouth on April 17.

On April 19 the *Albemarle* rammed and sank the USS *Smithfield*, damaged another wooden vessel and drove off still others.

Confederate forces, under the command of Robert F. Hoke, captured the town of Plymouth on April 20. Hoke was commissioned a Major General for his victory at Plymouth.

By April 26 Federal forces in North Carolina began to evacuate Washington following the fall of Plymouth.

On April 27 Major General Robert Hoke laid siege to Washington. There was a skirmish at Masonborough Inlet in new Hanover County.

William Ruffgun Cox, born in Scotland Neck, was promoted to Brigadier General in May 1864. Half of his troops in the Battle of Chancellorsville were killed or wounded.

On May 4 skirmishing flared on the Trent Road and south of the Trent River along Albemarle Sound; the Federals lost an outpost at Croatan.

Confederate forces failed in their attempt to retake New Bern on May 5. The CSS *Albemarle* engaged the Union squadron in the Roanoke River.

On May 11 one day before the Battle of Spotsylvania Courthouse, Colonel Thomas Miles Garrett remarked: "I will come out of this fight a Brigadier General or a dead Colonel." During the battle on the 12th, Garrett was killed and on the 13th, his commander received a dispatch from Richmond promoting him to Brigadier General. Garrett was born in Bertie County.

During the battle at Spotsylvania Courthouse, Brigadier General Junius Daniel was hit with a mini ball and died on the 13th. Daniel was born in Halifax, North Carolina.

In June William Gaston Lewis was promoted to Brigadier General, and his new command consisted of four North Carolina regiments and a battalion. Lewis was born in Rocky Mount on September 3, 1835.

The 66th North Carolina regiment from Wilmington saw their first action in Virginia on June 3 under Colonel Alexander Duncan Moore.

On June 16 Rufus Clay Barringer was promoted to the rank of Brigadier General. He was born in Cabarrus County December 2, 1821 and was one of the first to join the Confederate army after North Carolina seceded. Barringer fought in 76 actions and was wounded three times.

A small army-navy expedition by Federals on June 16 took five Confederate schooners near the mouth of the Pamlico River.

On June 20 a Federal expedition was carried out in and around Batchelder's Creek.

On June 22, a Federal scouting expedition probed from Piney Green to Snead's Ferry and Swansborough.

George Doherty Johnston, a native of Hillsborough, was promoted to Brigadier General on July 26. Johnston was making his home in Alabama at that time.

Jacob Hunter Sharp, a native of Hertford, was promoted to Brigadier General on July 28.

From July 28 to August 1 Federals carried out expeditions from New Bern to Manning's Neck.

The Confederate cruiser *Tallahassee* left the port of Wilmington for a three-week cruise, during which she took more than 30 prizes.

John Decatur Barry, a Wilmington native, was promoted to the temporary rank of Brigadier General on August 8.

Archibald Campbell Godwin, a native of Virginia, was sent to North Carolina by President Jefferson Davis to organize and construct a prison at Salisbury. On August 9 Godwin was promoted to Brigadier General but was killed in the battle of Winchester on September 19.

While camping near Petersburg, Virginia on August 24 Major Joseph Engelhard quoted General Robert E. Lee as saying of the North Carolina troops: "They stand as if they have tar on their heels."

On September 30 noted Confederate spy Rose O'Neal Greenhow drowned off Fort Fisher. She was buried at Oakdale cemetery in Wilmington.

In one of the most daring raids of the Civil War, William B. Cushing of the U.S. Navy rammed the *CSS Albemarle* with a torpedo, sinking her on October 27.

On November 5 William MacRae, a native of Wilmington who had been made a temporary Brigadier General in June, had the rank bestowed permanently.

The official report from the Confederate prison at Salisbury showed that they were housing over 8,500 prisoners in a facility built to house a maximum of 2,500.

On November 25 Robert Livingston, son of the famous missionary Dr. David Livingston, was killed in a riot at the Confederate prison in Salisbury.

Fifty-six warships of the United States Navy reached Fort Fisher off the coast of North Carolina on December 20.

The first attack on Fort Fisher occurred December 23. A novelty of the attack was the explosion of the Louisiana, an old powder vessel that was no longer serviceable. The explosion of the 615 tons of explosives did no damage to Fort Fisher.

From December 23-25 the U.S. Navy attacked Fort Fisher. On the 25th, Federal troops landed on the beach but were ordered to retreat by Union General Benjamin Butler as they approached the main part of the fort. This first attack upon the fort was a complete failure.

1865

The Union's 23rd Corp led by General Schofield arrived at Fort Fisher on January 9 to prepare for the attack on Wilmington.

On January 13 the attack upon Fort Fisher began and continued until the fort surrendered on January 15th.

On January 16 at Fort Fisher, two Union soldiers got drunk and as a result of their indiscretion, an extensive explosion destroyed the headquarters part of the Fort.

After the fall of Fort Fisher, Union troops moved across the Cape Fear River on January 16 and destroyed Forts Caswell, Holmes, Shaw and Campbell.

On January 28 General James G. Martin, leading a force comprised of infantry, artillery and cavalry, marched out of Wilmington to threaten the enemy's positions at Morehead City.

By February, General Martin was still trying to get to Morehead City but was being hampered by skirmishes at Gale's Creek and Bogue Sound. On February 3 General Martin received a dispatch ordering his return to Wilmington.

There were several skirmishes between the remaining Confederate forces and Union soldiers on February 17 at Smithville.

On February 17 T.A. Hall, Confederate inspector at the Salisbury prison, reported that conditions in the facility were very serious and that 3,000 prisoners had died there in the last four months.

Federal naval units bombarded Fort Anderson on the Cape Fear River on February 18. There was also some land action at Anderson and Orton Pond.

On February 18 General Robert E. Lee commissioned Collett Leventhorp to the rank of Brigadier General and ordered him to serve under General Braxton Bragg. For some unknown reason, Leventhorp declined the appointment on March 6.

Federal troops under Jacob D. Cox moved on February 19 to outflank Fort Anderson and the Confederate defense line on the west side of the Cape Fear River. Fighting broke out at Town Creek near Brunswick Town.

The Confederates, realizing that they could not hold Fort Anderson, abandoned it in the early morning hours of February 20.

On February 21 General Braxton Bragg ordered all troops under his command to evacuate Wilmington, thus closing the last port open to the Confederate government. Also on this day, skirmishes broke out at Eagle Island and Fort Strong across the Cape Fear River from Wilmington.

Federal forces moved into Wilmington on February 21 and columns of smoke could be seen as the Confederates began destroying their stores. By nightfall, all Confederates had left the city and the Union forces declared the city taken on the 22nd.

Realizing that the end was near, officials at the Confederate prison in Salisbury exchanged 2, 871 Union prisoners on February 22.

Skirmishes were held on Smith's Creek and Northeast Ferry just north of Wilmington on February 22.

On February 23 Paul Roberts, a native of Gates County, was promoted to Brigadier General.

Confederate forces took the ironclad *Chickamauga* up the Cape Fear River to scuttle her on February 25.

General Robert E. Lee placed General Joseph Johnston in command of all forces in the Carolinas on February 25.

On March 4 there was a skirmish at Phillip's Crossroads and the U.S. transport Thorn was destroyed by a torpedo in the Cape Fear River near Fort Anderson.

General William T. Sherman's troops entered North Carolina on March 7 with skirmishes at Rockingham and Southwest Creek.

A new battle of Kinston and Wise's Forks began on March 8. Heavy fighting continued on the 9th between General Braxton Bragg and Union General Jacob Cox.

On March 9 Confederate cavalry under Generals Wade Hampton and Joe Wheeler attacked and surprised the Federal cavalry at Monroe's Crossroads. Union General Judson Kilpatrick was nearly captured in his bed. He managed to escape but without his pants. Later the affair was called "The Battle of Kilpatrick's Pants."

General W.H.C. Whiting, wounded in the battle of Fort Fisher, was taken to Fort Columbus, New York where he died on March 10.

On March 12 Sherman's troops took over the Cumberland County Courthouse at Fayetteville.

Sherman's forces at Fayetteville carried out reconnaissance to Black River and Silver Run Creek on March.

Sherman's army left Fayetteville on March 15. The Union cavalry skirmished heavily with rear guards of Confederate troops at Smith's Mill on Black River.

During the battle of Aversboro, from March 15th to 16th, John Smith's home "Oak Grove" was used as a Confederate hospital; two days later, it was seized and used as a Union hospital. As a result of the Aversboro battle, the Federals had 95 killed, 533 wounded and 54 missing. The total Confederate losses were 865.

In mid-March a squad of Union cavalry carried off 19 black men from Monroe in Union County; 13 escaped and returned home.

Fayetteville began preparations for Sherman's arrival when word reached the town on March 10 that he was marching in its direction.

General Sherman's second step in his march to the sea came to a successful halt on March 11 with his occupation of Fayetteville. He sent word to General Schofield in Wilmington that he had taken Fayetteville.

Sherman's army remained in Fayetteville on March 12 to destroy army machinery, buildings and other property deemed of use to the Confederate forces.

As an aftermath of Aversboro, there was skirmishing in the area and at Falling Creek, N.C. on March 17.

On March 18 both Generals Joseph Johnston and Wade Hampton made plans for the next day's attack at Bentonville.

The Battle of Bentonville started on March 19 and lasted for three days. Casualties for the Federals were listed at 1,500 and for the Confederates, 2,600. These casualties of 4,100 made this the worst single man-made disaster in North Carolina's history.

On March 23 there were several skirmishes at Cox's Bridge on the Neuse River.

Aboard the River Queen at City Point, Virginia on March 27, President Lincoln, General Grant and General Sherman discussed Sherman's victories in the Carolinas. Sherman returned to Goldsboro on the 29th.

There were skirmishes near Snow Hill on March 28.

Stoneman's Union cavalry moved into western North Carolina near Boon on March 28. Within a twenty-four hour period, Stoneman's forces were fighting around Wilkesborough.

There were skirmishes at Snow Hill and near Goldsboro on April 1-2.

On April 2 James Edmond Boyd, a courier at Appomattox, carried the message from General Lee to General Grant requesting a meeting to arrange for surrender. Boyd was born in Orange County.

There was a Union expedition in and around Asheville on April 3. Though the fighting continued until the 6th, no deaths were reported.

On April 5 the Confederates burned two Federal steamers near Maple Cypress and Cowpen Landing.

On April 10 Sherman's army left their campgrounds at Smithfield and headed to Raleigh.

The Confederate government, fearing Stoneman's forces in the west, moved to Greensboro on April 10. At Greensboro on the 12th, President Davis met with General Johnston; Johnston recommended negotiations but Davis said only surrender would be accepted. Most of those present sided with Johnston so Davis gave him the power to negotiate with Sherman.

On April 12 the Confederate prison at Salisbury that once housed over 10,000 prisoners, was destroyed. Sherman's Army continued its march on Raleigh.

At Salisbury on April 12, Stoneman's Federal cavalry captured 1,300 Confederates.

From April 12-15 President Jefferson Davis held his last cabinet meeting in Greensboro.

General Sherman made his grand entry into Raleigh on April 13. Only one soldier was killed in the surrender of Raleigh: Lt. Welsh of the 11th Texas Cavalry who was hung at Lovejoy's Grove (now site of the Governor's Mansion).

On April 14-15, there were skirmishes at Morrisville and Chapel Hill.

On April 15 President Davis left Greensboro for Charlotte. He arrived in Lexington on the 16th and was encouraged to move on, reaching Salisbury on the 17th and Concord on the 18th.

General Sherman left Raleigh on April 17 to meet with General Johnston. Before he left, he received the telegram telling of Lincoln's assassination. He held the telegraph operator to secrecy until he returned to Raleigh. Four thousand Union cavalry forces entered Chapel Hill and took over the town on the same day.

On April 18 Johnston and Sherman signed a "memorandum or basis of agreement." Johnston surrendered his 37,000 troops and except for the western part of the state, all fighting in North Carolina ceased.

President Davis reached Charlotte on April 19 and heard of Lincoln's assassination. On the 26th, he met with his cabinet and agreed to leave and go west of the Mississippi. Attorney General George Davis disagreed with those plans and left for his home in Wilmington.

On April 22 there were skirmishes at Howard's Gap in the Blue Ridge Mountains.

Stoneman's Federal cavalry saw action in Hendersonville on April 23.

General U.S. Grant visited Raleigh on April 24 to confer with General Sherman on the terms of surrender with General Johnston. General Grant left Raleigh on the 29th.

General Sherman and General Johnston met at the Bennett House near Durham on April 26; Johnston formally surrendered his forces.

On May 6 General James G. Martin surrendered the Army of Western North Carolina, the last Confederate forces in North Carolina.

On May 8 Colonel J.R. Love led his Confederate forces against the Union cavalry in western North Carolina. This was the last battle of the Civil War in North Carolina. On May 9th the last Confederate soldier, a North Carolinian, was killed at Waynesville.

Governor Zebulon B. Vance was arrested on May 13 and sent to Washington where he was held prisoner for two months.

On May 29 President Andrew Johnson appointed William W. Holden provisional governor of North Carolina.

On June 1 the Confederate reports showed that North Carolina lost a total of 40, 275 men in the Civil War.

President Andrew Johnson appointed James Johnson, a native of Robeson County, as provisional governor of Georgia.

On August 9 an epidemic of smallpox broke out in Wilmington.

On October 5 an ordinance was passed that permanently prohibited slavery in North Carolina.

North Carolina ratified the 13th Amendment to the Constitution (abolishment of slavery) on December 18.

Records of Oakdale Cemetery in Wilmington indicate that there are 550 Confederate soldiers buried in the Confederate lot. Further, there are 380 graves scattered throughout other areas of this cemetery and in Bellevue, the Roman Catholic cemetery. There are nearly 100 more soldiers buried in private burial grounds in the Wilmington area.

The Wilmington Soldiers Aid Society held the first Memorial Service to the Confederate dead on July 21, 1866.

The impressive bronze memorial statue in memory of Confederate heroes was unveiled on May 10, 1872 at Oakdale Cemetery.

A stone was placed on the grave of Rose Greenhow, a Confederate spy who is buried in Oakdale Cemetery, in 1897.

About The Author

J.C. Knowles is the President of the Apex Downtown Business Association, Apex Town Ambassador, and Editor and Publisher "The Gazette."

J. C. is the official Ambassador of Apex, North Carolina. He was also Apex Citizen of the Year in 2007 & 2014. He is a publisher, writer, auctioneer for 44 years (retired) and a North Carolina Historian.

In addition he is a member of the Apex Rotary Club, Swift Creek Exchange Club and Raleigh Kiwanis Club.

J.C. served on the Raleigh/Wake County School Board 15 years, was on the North Carolina Historical Commission for six years, and on the President Andrew Johnson Commission for 10 years.

He has a great love of history and publishes historical tidbits daily.

He also has taught over 50,000 school children about the history of North Carolina.

CPSIA information can be obtained
at www.ICGtesting.com
Printed in the USA
JSHW021936291220
10521JS00005B/152